THE CROOKED PATH JOURNAL

The Crooked Path Journal
A Discourse on the Nameless Art

⁂ In This Issue ⁂

Letters from the Editor *by Raven Womack*	3
Black *by Krystal Raven)o(*	9
Oak *by Ellen Evert Hopman*	11
Born of the Fires of Other and Self *by Lucera Fumaltera*	18
Which Way Did She Go? *by Crowstar*	27
Spotlight: "The Crooked Path Apothecary" *by Raven Womack*	29
Magick as Dwelling in Truth *by Alecto Aletheia Hypatia*	35
The Gods Are Not Your New Toys *by Mark NeCamp*	43
On the Making of Magical Tools *by John Breen*	49
A Poem *by J.P. Sedgewick*	57
Paganism, Diversity, and the Pandemic *by Kelsey Pullaro*	59
To Kindle the Magickal Flame *by Ilana Sturm*	63
Sacred Boundaries in Pagan Practice *by Pegi Eyers*	69
Of Wine and Sabbats *by Hillary Klein*	75
Language of the Mind *by Soledad Osraige*	89
Journey to the Castle (an excerpt) *by Ann Finnin*	93

© Pendraig Publishing, Inc 2021
All contributors retain copyright to their individual works.
All rights reserved. No part of this publication may be reproduced or utilized in any form or by any means, electronic or mechanical, including photocopying, recording, or be any information storage and retrieval system, prior consent of the copyright holder and publisher except brief quotations used in review.
The authors and publisher assume no responsibility for any errors or omission. This book is not intended as a substitute for medical advice. No liability is assumed for damages that may result from the use of information contained within.

ISBN 978-1-936922-95-6
Editor: Raven Womack
Contributing Editor: Monica Castillo
Cover Design: Ted Venemann
Pendraig Publishing, Inc
PO Box 8427 Green Valley Lake CA 92341 USA
www.pendraigpublishing.com

For the Cunningman with the exquisite hats...

Letters from the Editor

Part 1:

Introduction

The Crooked Path – A Journal of the Nameless Art, is a legacy from our founder Peter Paddon. The last issue, published in the winter of 2011, was number 7. It was, of course, to be followed by issue number 8, but for whatever reason – and likely there were many – that never came to be.

When I first took over Pendraig Publishing after Peter's untimely and unexpected passing, I truly had no idea what a tremendous undertaking managing a small publishing company was, and it has taken some years to get my footing. Well, I'm not altogether sure I really have my footing just yet, but I have made some progress over the years, learning book layout, publishing lingo and how to navigate the sometimes tenuous and sometimes nebulous relationship Pagan authors have with accepted standards of capitalization; by this, I mean I have learned to acquiesce in relationship to standards in favor of consistency. Perhaps the best achievement is that we've actually gotten a few books to press and they are all doing well. Until this year, I had never really wanted to try my hand at The Crooked Path, but for whatever reason I decided that this was the year to resurrect the Journal. I didn't make this decision alone or lightly, of course. I conferred with the editorial staff – that's me, Luna, and

Linda – and together we decided to bring the Journal back, but with some tweaks - some changes here and there. Okay, some of these changes are pretty significant.

Our first decision was to change publication from quarterly to biannually - four times a year just seemed way too daunting to me, but this could change later. Our next change was instead of focusing mainly on Pendraig authors, we decided to open it up to anyone, even authors with other publishing houses. We all agree that Pagan publishing is hard enough, and we think that it would be awesome if the many small publishing companies worked together and supported each other. Another significant change is that each issue would have a theme and that the themes should be a little broader reaching.

By broader reaching, I mean that the themes should encompass the many social, cultural, and political issues that we all have to deal with on a mundane as well as a magickal level. Let's face it, we live in interesting times - uneasy, volatile, rapidly changing times. While many of these issues affect our mundane lives in varying ways, we can not separate their effects from our magickal lives and communities. The issues of politics, anti-scientism, cultural appropriation, racism, religious fundamentalism, gender issues, white supremacy, nationalism, feminism, etc….all of these issues affect our Pagan and magickal communities and sometimes manifest in very ugly ways. So, each publication will have a theme that deals with a specific issue, and some of these issues will be difficult ones. I don't expect everyone to agree but rest assured, all reasonable voices will be considered. The editorial staff doesn't have to agree with the viewpoint of a submission, but as you can imagine, there will be certain limitations as to what we'll publish. No hate speech, bullying or personal attacks will be published.

A lot of these issues are debated ad hominem online on various social media platforms, but there seems to be a real downside to this. While social media has in many ways made communication and the exchange of ideas easier, it certainly lacks a certain nuance, and it has definitely allowed for discussions to become very one-sided. I've watched as debates turn into ridiculous character assassinations that are more akin to bullying than an exchange of information or ideas. "Witch Wars", have always been a bane of our existence - have now been taken to new and vicious heights through our keyboard warriorism.

Not all articles and essays will deal with the theme, but we're striving for at least 50% of the content to be theme related. We'll still be publishing articles on herbs, rituals, folklore, and the other standard fare as well as excerpts from books currently or soon to be in publication.

Another change will be the addition of "regular features". One such feature will be "Letters to the Editor." If a particular article or essay stirs you to write a reply or a rebuttal, we're making space for that. Again, there will be limits to what we'll publish, but a certain amount of space will be allotted in each issue for such letters. Another regular feature will be to spotlight a Pagan/Magickal/Occult business. I know from experience how hard it is to run a Pagan business so if we can in some small way support our local businesses, we are happy to do so.

All of our changes in form, format and features are fluid. I have always preferred to let things evolve in an organic kind of way. But there is one revision that will forever change The Journal. There have been seven issues of The Crooked Path: A Journal of the Nameless Art and when we decided to go forward with a new issue, we naturally assumed that it would be the eighth issue in the series. But on reflection I feel that this is really a new beginning – a new volume. So, welcome to:

The Crooked Path Journal: A Discourse on the Nameless Art, Volume II, Issue 1

Part II:

In this Issue: Diversity, Privilege and Cultural Appropriation in the Pagan Community

The whole process of rebirthing The Crooked Path Journal really got its deciding spark when I watched the attempted destruction of a Pagan author's reputation by a much younger, *fake woke* individual on social media. I probably would have "gotten out the popcorn" to watch the back and forth if I hadn't been so aghast at the virulent and aggressive attack on a woman for expressing her support for a Dianic group's decision to not allow transwomen into their circles and rituals. The attack was framed as being in support of our trans brothers and sisters, but it turned out that the initiator of the attack had some mud on her shoes as well in regard to her treatment and attitudes towards trans folks in the past. While trying to portray this aggression as a "public service announcement", the instigator also asked for "receipts" of anti-trans statements as well as racist statements by said author. This was, in my opinion, a very underhanded way to imply that the author being derided was also a racist. No one could provide any proof of that but of course the implication was already out there. I suspect, I mean I strongly suspect, like deep in my gut, that the real motive was really something else altogether and to be honest, the author being attacked was a Pendraig author so you could say that I had a vested interest in the outcome. It took everything I had to not chime in on the discussion, but maybe not for the reason you might think.

The TERF Wars as they are sometimes called had gotten my attention before. For those unfamiliar with the term, TERF stands for "trans-exclusionary radical feminist." This is not a Pagan term but a radical feminist term that has carried over into Pagandom. Basically, and I do mean very basically, in Paganism the issue is that some Dianic witches don't allow transwomen to join their rituals, circles and groups. This issue first got my attention a few years ago at once very popular and well attended Pagan convention in California when a Dianic group not only excluded transwomen from a scheduled women's event but announced it in the program. A very peaceful and well-done protest occurred in response, but many people were torn as to what side of the issue was the right side and while some people were outraged, a lot of people were just sad.

It made me sad when I read the reports, blogs, and eye-witness reports of the people who were there. While I am neither a Dianic witch nor am I transwoman, I could feel the pain and anguish of people on both sides of the issue. So, when this whole social media war started, I refrained from commenting on either side of the issue for a couple of reasons. For one thing, as previously mentioned I felt like there was really another motive for the attack, but also because I can really see both sides of the issue. In fact, I tried to write an article on just that issue but try as I may I just couldn't get it right. I don't have a side; I understand both arguments. I could literally argue for either side. In truth, I feel that this issue is so emotional for those involved even not taking a side will probably get me in hot water. I will say that every Dianic witch I spoke to expressed their support for trans rights but still insisted that didn't mean that they had a right to be in their Dianic circles. Every trans-witch I spoke to didn't accept the reasons that Dianics give for not including them. Let's face it, it's a complicated issue.

As I pondered the issue and watched this vapid witch war play out, it occurred to me that of all the communities, and I use that term loosely, that Pagans are perhaps one of if not the most diverse groups of people there is. Under the vast umbrella of Paganism are people that follow many different gods, in many different ways and practice many different types of magick with a vast assortment of philosophies, theologies and cultural roots. Many consider Paganism to be an alternative lifestyle yet within Paganism you will find a plethora of "other" alternative lifestyles being lived by people with various and sundry sexual preferences, gender identities and races.

The diversity of traditions, pantheons, ritual practices, and the acceptance of that diversity is something I have always loved about being Pagan. When I had my store in North Hollywood, I always tried to be open to that wonderful, chaotic diversity. We sought out and welcomed people of many divergent paths to present classes and rituals. Sexual preference, gender identity, race or alternative lifestyles were never an issue. All were welcome as long as they respected the paths of others. Or were they? I can't help but wonder if I simply had on rose-colored glasses. If I were a Black, lesbian witch, that attended Raven's Flight rituals, would I have felt welcome and accepted? When our annual Witches Ball had a Day of the Dead theme, were we disrespecting the Mexican culture?

How do the issues of racism, LGBTQIA+ rights, white privilege, women's rights, and indigenous rights affect us as Pagans? How do these issues manifest in the Pagan community? It's foolish and naïve to think that these very human issues don't carry over. My "reality" as a white, cis gender Pagan woman may differ greatly from Pagans of other races, sexual orientations, or gender identities. As a witch, as a cunning woman, I know how nebulous reality can be and I wonder if I've been arrogant or oblivious to how others might view the state of things in the Pagan world.

On the other hand, can we be trying so hard to be correct that we're not seeing the forest for the trees A dear friend, who's a very manly man, was excluded one year from that same California convention I mentioned earlier because he was too masculine. This is the same event where years ago, we performed a powerful and ecstatic Horned God ritual where men were actually weeping because we were celebrating the masculine where main priest of that rite was a gay man.

Then there's the very big issue of cultural appropriation. That's a huge ball of wax right there. When is it appropriation and when is it simply following your heart, or using what works? Have some of us swung the pendulum so far in the other direction trying to be better and trying to be more sensitive to the issues that we've become insensitive to other issues? Should white people who practice Hoodoo be excluded from events due to cultural appropriation? Do we quit using white sage even though the vast majority of what's sold today is commercially grown? Do all the white people who've been working with the Egyptian gods for years, have to stop? I've even heard it going around that only Roma people can read tarot cards because it's their culture and if anyone else does it, it's appropriation. Where is the line? Can we exclude the white Hoodoo practitioner but keep our tarot cards?

In my experience, pretty much every Wiccan or witchcraft tradition being practiced today is a combination of bits and pieces of various practices and cultures. Hell, even our precious Wheel of the Year is conglomeration of rites from different cultures. I have yet to see evidence of one culture that celebrated all eight of the sabbats. Do we deconstruct our traditions, rites and rituals and try to sanitize them of all cultural references, roots, and aspects that we weren't born into? And then what are we left with? I suspect that the eventual demise of that once great Pagan gathering was caused to a great extent by this trend of trying too hard to be too politically correct. In years past you could go to Norse oracular ritual one night, an Umbanda ecstatic ritual the next, and the next day maybe participate in a Dianic circle, or attend an raucous ritual celebrating masculine divinity, a class on Faery traditions or take a guided meditation into the underworld. It was always about diversity and exploring other paths, learning new things and finding your niche or just exploring new ones, but it seems to have morphed into an event where only approved diversity was allowed. Of course, it's the prerogative of any event organizing staff to mold their event into their vision but is that really what we want our greater Pagan community to become? A rigid formula of wokeness that would force people to give up their traditions, rites and maybe even their gods? Do we demonize the Dianics but not the Radical Faeries?

Personally, I don't give fuck all about what's under your skirt or not in your pants. I don't care who you love or what god you pray to no matter what color your skin is, where you were raised or what DNA you possess. If I had a women's ritual, I would gladly welcome transwomen but that's me and my path. I certainly would not demonize or try to ruin someone for walking their own or for standing up for those who choose to follow theirs. Of course, some will say that's my privilege talking.

These are complicated issues in the greater world at large but it would seem that these issues have many more layers of complexity when it comes to our Pagan communities and practices. As we all strive to be better humans, to be more inclusive, to be more respectful and believe me, I think we should be all of those things, how do we decide or know how to translate that into our lives as Pagans? Is it all or nothing or is there some middle ground?

So, that's why I chose these topics, this theme for this inaugural issue of the new Crooked Path Journal. We put out the call for submissions that addressed these issues, and we received some wonderful articles from some very talented and passionate writers. We won't solve it all today, but hopefully if we try listening to each other and not always needing to be right, we might begin to understand each other a little and maybe find a way for us all to find our place under this big, convoluted umbrella known as Paganism.

Black

By Raven Krystal)o(

Just the word "Black," by itself with no context, conjures images of shadows, horned creatures, the terror of the unknown, and more. Applied to magick, the word doubles down on such themes, creating stereotypes associated with evil, hatred, and death. As a daughter of both Black Culture and Black Magick, I am uniquely pressed by these fear-based traditions from all sides. People who do not understand what it means to be of Blackness in magick or culture often assume that those of Black skin or black garb are dangerous, inherently violent, or somehow inferior. As a Black woman, I have experienced white women immediately fearing me for simply being present. As a Pagan Satanist, I have experienced Black women immediately fearing me for simply being present. The parallels between these two forms of otherization are vast and poignant. Satanism has several popular forms, but the most widespread and well-known version in the United States is actually not about that red guy with hooves from the underworld. LaVeyan Satanists believe that all deities are strictly mythological and that by practicing forms of "self-worship," one can achieve higher states of consciousness. Most LaVeyan Satanists do not believe in an afterlife of any kind, so they do not believe in Hell or Heaven. I find this version of Satanism to have many positive qualities, including how compatible it is with Atheism. The more ways we have to connect those without theistic worldviews to the experience of Universal Oneness, the better, in my personal opinion. Pagan Satanism is very different from LaVeyan Satanism. Foremost, we are often theists who have personally experienced the presence of the Divine in some way. Since the rise of Christianity, all deities with horns, tails, hooves, dark wings, red/black skin, or affiliations with the underworld have been collectively acknowledged by one word: Satan. Since the enslavement of generations of Black people and the annihilation of hundreds of Native American tribes in the United States, all non-colonized rituals have been labeled taboo, dangerous, evil, primitive, or Satanic. For a Pagan Satanist, the moniker "Satan" is shorthand for "all misunderstood and maligned deities of the Old Ways." Likewise, the word "Hell" is just a nickname for all the forms of the underworld that Christianity bundled up and melted into "a lake that burns with fire and brimstone." When approaching another culture's deities as a Pagan Satanist, the very first step is to understand that you are an outsider. We fully acknowledge that our worldview has been colored by a forced homogenization of concepts and images that were stolen from around the world and then mass denigrated into our beloved and much maligned Horned God. At no time do we seek ownership or authority over the Divine, so it follows that at no time do we seek ownership or authority over someone else's interpretation of the Divine. When we feel a strong connection to a particular culture, deity, ritual, or tradition, it is then our job to learn everything we can about that thing from those who have lived it in their experiences. Then, when we have mastered the connection, we show gratitude to those who guided us on this journey. In these ways, we respect other cultures as we learn to create our own.

I am Black. I am a Satanist. I am not a threat.

About the Author

Since the 1990s, Raven Krystal has been exploring the occult, shamanic wisdom, and other mystery schools related to cracking the secrets of the universe. She has been initiated as a Pristess of several persuassions, is a renowned ritualist, and has a reputation as a passionate activist for human and animal rights. Her experiences with end of life processes and the paranormal have led her to serve as a death midwife and grief minister in the international Pagan community.

Patreon:)O(The Krustal Raven)O(

Oak

Excerpt from: Tree Medicine, Tree Magic
(Pendraig Publishing Inc, 2017)

by Ellen Evert Hopman

Faerie-folk are in Old Oaks

I am blessed to be living in an oak forest in Western Massachusetts. They line my driveway and stand outside my kitchen door. It is to them that I owe the inspiration for the book Tree Medicine Tree Magic.

As a professional herbalist, I maintain several small patches of medicinal herbs around the house. My clients and students are often directed to local supermarkets and herbariums to buy healing herbs, and this can be a frustrating experience. Growing conditions in my area are such that winter will force people to depend on commercial establishments unless they have dried herbs from a summer garden. What a joy to discover that certain trees, such as the oak, are available year-round.

***

Several years ago, my love of Celtic music and dance led me to the study of Celtic mysticism. I quickly became fascinated by the Druids; those legendary poet-priests of pre-Christian Europe. The available literature yielded an important insight; because the Celts lived as far south as Portugal and Spain, and as far east as Russia, almost anyone with European blood was bound to have Celtic ancestors. This made the Celts kin of mine and therefore worthy of serious study.

When many of us think of Druids, one image stands out - the vision of the sacred grove of oaks. Why did our ancestors value this tree so highly? Could it be that trees which were extremely valuable for survival became associated with the power of the Gods? Our ancestors were also sensitive to the spiritual qualities that could be felt in the presence of an oak tree.

One day while in meditation, I was inspired to get up and hug a nearby tree. It occurred to me with overwhelming certainty that this tree was the "royal protector" of the surrounding area.

It was standing sentinel, protecting local vegetation and animals, and only when I lifted my eyes to its branches did, I realize that this mighty spirit was an oak.

The word "Druid" may be derived from the Celtic "derw" (oak), and "ydd" (a part of), which combine to form "Derwydd," an ancient term for the Celtic class of learned experts. The Druids may have chosen oak as their favorite tree because of its strength and endurance. This tree has roots that are at least as deep as its branches are high, with a strong, stout trunk to channel the forces of Earth and Sky. Oaks are often struck by lightning and survive, thus symbolizing a spirituality which is well grounded but that reaches for the heights.

Oaks have an honored place in the hearts and minds of the people of Britain; an island that was once covered with vast oak forests. According to tradition, Arthur's Round Table was made from the single slab of an oak tree. Trees of up to thirty-six feet in diameter have been recorded as growing in British soil.

Avoid oaks during thunderstorms as they tend to draw lightning.

Practical Uses

The oak is considered the finest building material because it is strong and flexible. It is a very dense hardwood and is an excellent heating fuel. Oak bark is also rich in tannic acid which makes it ideal for tanning hides.

Oak bark mixed with additives produces various dyes for cloth. Iron salts added to oak bark make a black dye; alum salts a brown dye and tin salts, or zinc salts a yellow dye. The inner bark of the Black Oak will create yellow on alum mordanted wool, gold with the addition of chrome and olive green with copperas. Silk will dye orange. With the addition of copperas, the English Oak colors wool black.

Acorns were, until recently, a prime fodder for pigs, and were also used as a staple food for humans before wheat was introduced. Most acorns are extremely bitter and need to be leached in a running stream (Or in the refrigerator! Pour off and replace the water every day for two weeks) or repeatedly boiled in hot water before they can be eaten like nuts or ground into flour. Their nutritional components are 6.3 percent water, 5.2 % protein, 43 % fat, and 45 % carbohydrate. The acorns of the White Oak are the most palatable and required very little leaching.

Herbal Uses

* The ideas, procedures and suggestions in this article are not meant to replace the medical advice of a trained medical professional. All matters regarding your health require medical supervision. Consult your physician before adopting any of the suggestions in this book as well about any condition that may require diagnosis or medical attention. Any applica- tions of the treatments set forth in this book are at the reader's discretion. The author and publisher disclaim any liability arising directly or indirectly from the use of this book.

Oaks are known as astringent tonics, meaning they will shrink, tone, and heal tissues. A tea made from the bark is used as an enema for hemorrhoids or as a douche for vaginitis. It will benefit bloody urine, stop internal hemorrhages, reduce fevers, and soothe sore throats. Oak bark tea may be used internally and externally to shrink varicose veins, and as a wash for sores and skin irritations. It has been used as a hair rinse to stop hair loss and dandruff.

Culpeper advises using an infusion of the leaves for douching and a tea of the bark to check diarrhea. Sebastian Kniepp says a cloth dipped into a decoction of the fresh or dried bark can be wrapped around the neck to heal goiters and glandular inflammations. He also recommends a sitz-bath (four inches of tea in the bathtub) plus occasional enemas for prolapse of the rectum and fistulas as well as tumors of the rectal area.

The leaves (when gathered before summer solstice) and inner bark are used together as a dressing for burns. The acorns and inner bark of the White Oak are made into a decoction and added to milk to counteract the side effects of harsh medicines, especially when the bladder has been damaged, and there is blood in the urine.

White Oak inner bark, taken as a tea, helps clean the body of excess mucus caused by sinus congestion, postnasal drip, and lung congestion. It also improves the stomach's ability to absorb and secrete substances.

Collect the inner bark of branches and twigs.

To make the tea, place one tablespoon of inner bark in one pint of water and simmer for ten minutes. Drink up to three cups per day, between meals. For enemas and douches, simmer one tablespoon of bark in one quart of water for thirty minutes, then strain and use the fluid.

"Spiritus Glandium Quercus" and "Aqua Glandium Quercus" are homeopathic preparations made from peeled acorns and used to treat alcoholism, bad breath, constipation, diarrhea, splenic dropsy, fistula, dizziness, gout, intermittent fever, leukemia, and splenic conditions.

Dr. Edward Bach, the inventor of flower essence therapy, prescribed the flower essence of oak for those people who experience despondency and despair, yet keep on trying. These people never seem to give up hope and are disappointed if an illness keeps them from their work. They enjoy helping others and may over- work themselves, hiding their tiredness so as not to disturb anyone. They are patient, strong, and endowed with common sense. When healthy, they reflect perseverance, courage, and stability.

Magical Uses

Not surprisingly, there is a wealth of magical lore dealing with the oak. It is a tree ruled by the Sun, associated with the element Fire, and it bestows the qualities of protection, healing, financial success, sexual potency, fertility and general good luck.

Several books recommend making an equal armed solar cross out of oak twigs tied together with a red ribbon to protect against evil.

Carrying a piece of oak will offer protection.

Acorns are powerful magical tools as well. They can be placed in a window to ward off lightning, carried to prevent illness and pain, and worn as talismans of fertility, immortality, and longevity. Plant one in the dark of the Moon to induce financial prosperity.

Because acorns are symbolic of immortality and the continuity of life, they are especially appropriate to the "Samhain" or Hallowe'en season. Use them as ornaments and to decorate altars in the fall.

Oak branches were traditionally burned in midsummer fires and used to make wands and staves. Topping the wand with an acorn will help in fertility rituals. The working of positive magic will be enhanced if the wood for wands is gathered during the waxing Moon. Be sure to leave an appropriate gift as an exchange.

An old custom advises, to help in healing a wound, that you take a dressing that has been on the injured body part, sprinkle it with oil of rue, and place it inside the hollow of an oak tree during the waning Moon. The wound will be transferred through the tree to the ground and dispersed into the earth.

When gathering leaves, acorns, or branches of oak, it is fitting to honor the old custom of "feeding the oak" by pouring a libation of spirits upon the roots. Acorns are best gathered by day and leaves and wood by night. Oaks should only be cut down during the waning Moon. A few days before cutting the tree, take the time to tell it what you are about to do. You can plant an acorn near the old tree so that the tree spirit will have a new home.

The Gaelic word for oak is "duir" from which we have the word "door." A "door" is both a gateway and protection from outside influences. The oak opens the door to a strong spiritual focus that can survive the tests and ordeals of time.

The Latin for oak is "quercus" from the Celtic "quer" (fine) and "cuez" (tree). The Quercus species is sacred to the Dagda, Dianus, Jupiter, Thor, Zeus, Hercules, Herne, Janus, Rhea, Cerridwen, Cernunnos, Cybele, Hecate, Pan, Erato, Bridget, Blodeuwedd, and Odin. For those inclined towards the Old Religion, the burning of powdered oak bark as incense is an appropriate offering for any of these Gods. Oaks are part of the sacred triad of "Oak and Ash and Thorn." The Celts were very partial to the number three, and where these three trees grew together it was said one was likely to see fairies.

Twylah Nitsch, of the Seneca tribe, in her book Language of the Trees, has published a nice introduction to the Native American perception of the symbolism of trees. To the Seneca nation, the oak, with its aura of reserved power, is a tree of strength - a strength that is the result of decades of steady growth. The oak conveys a sense of structure and solidity, and it symbolizes self-discipline, awareness and high ideals.

The Seneca tribe sensed that trees could be used as tools for personal growth and as a mirror for defining individuals. Oak people are felt to be motivators and creative thinkers with an efficient eye for detail. They project reliability, gentle firmness, and sincerity. Strong and silent, these people are spiritually inclined and derive inner strength from taking the time to center themselves. They trust in their intuition and listen carefully to their inner voices.

Druidic Insights

As a practicing Druid for over thirty years, oaks are one of my most important spiritual allies. These trees are the ultimate symbol of balance; their roots go down as deep as the tree is tall, and they are as potent a talisman for a Druid as a cross would be for a Christian.

Oaks are generous beings; giving their firewood to warm us and their heartwood for our homes. Their leaves and inner bark make medicine for the sick and their acorns provide sustenance for people and animals. This generosity of spirit is what a Druid seeks to emulate; being so balanced and successful in the world that one can help others.

Oaks also have the ability to attract lightning, or the attention of the Sky Gods and not get blasted; this too is the ambition of the Druid. We seek to commune with the high gods even as we stay focused on our mundane practical life.

The ancient Indo-European word for oak *deru- has bequeathed words like "door" and "durable" to us. Oak is indeed a doorway between the worlds when we travel shamanically down to the underworld of the Sidhe (Fairy) realms through the roots or up to the celestial realm of the gods through its branches.

The strength of oak is a grounding shield for our spirit as we travel between the worlds.

About the Author

Ellen Evert Hopman is a Master Herbalsit and lay homeopath who holds an M.Ed. in Mental Health Counseling. She is a registered herbalist in the American Herbalists Guild. Hopman is a founding member of The Order of the White Oak (Ord Na Darach Gile, http://www.whiteoakdruids.org) and its former Co-Chief. She is a Bard of the Gorsedd of Caer Abiri, and an Archdruidess of the Druid Clan of Dana (Grove of Brighid).Ellen is currently Archdruid of the Tribe of the Oak, a Celtic Reconstructionist, international teaching Grove of Druids, https://tribeoftheoak.com/. She was Vice President of the Henge of Keltria, an interantional Druid Fellowhip, for nine years and has been at times a member of The Order of Bards, Ovates and Druids and of Ar nDraiocht Fein: A Druid Fellowship (ADF).

Books by Ellen Evert Hopman

The Sacred Herbs of Spring – Magical Healing and Edible Plants to Celebrate Beltaine (Destiny Books, 2020)

The Sacred Herbs of Samhain – Plants to Communicate with the Spirits of the Dead (Destiny Books, 2019)

The Real Witches of New England – History, Lore and Modern Practice (Destiny books, 2018),

Tree Medicine Tree Magic – revised and updated (Pendraig Publishing, 2017)

A Legacy of Druids - Conversations with Druid leaders of Britain, the USA and Canada, past and present (Moon Books, 2016),

Secret Medicines from your Garden – Plants for Healing, Spirituality, and Magic (Healing Arts Press, 2016), Winner of the Thomas DeBaggio Annual Book Award of the International Herb Association (2016) and also a Coalition of Visionary Resources winner in 2016.

Scottish Herbs and Fairy Lore (Pendraig Publishing, June, 2011),

The Secret Medicines of Your Kitchen (mPowr Ltd., London, October 2012),

A Druid's Herbal of Sacred Tree Medicine, (9781594772306), Destiny Books, June 2008,

Priestess of the Forest: A Druid Journey (Llewellyn, February 2008, re-released from Oak Spirit Publishing 2021)

The Druid Isle (Llewellyn, April 2010, re-released from Oak Spirit Publishing 2021),

Priestess of the Fire Temple: A Druid's Tale (Llewellyn, March, 2012, re-released from Oak Spirit Publishing 2021),

Walking the World in Wonder - A Children's Herbal (Healing Arts Press, 2000),

Being a Pagan: Druids, Wiccans, and Witches Today (9780892819041), Destiny Books, 2001.

A Druid's Herbal for the Sacred Earth Year (Destiny Books, 1994)

See Ellen Evert Hopman's books and blog at www.elleneverthopman.com Study Druidism with her at Tribe of the Oak www.tribeoftheoak.com

Born of the Fires of Other and Self

By Lucera Fumaltera

completed on the Dark Moon, March 2021

> "All through my trances as a recurrent motif is a being that I know as "The Other." It is as familiar and as near to me, as myself – in fact, it seems to be a complementary part of my self, separate yet united with me."
>
> ~Rosaleen Norton[1]

Many of us may feel we do not truly belong to any one path; we may connect with the literature about traditions and practices that have been around for centuries – but may not be connected to our home, our heritage, or our praxis. Because of this separation, the feeling of isolation is underscored for the Solitary. Once we have been exposed to the mysteries of esoteric connection, we are forever changed. This is my forsaken experience with being Witched, with Them (whatever this means for you), and as a Solitary, miles from connections other than Other.

We practice our crafts, fine-tuning every affect and practically and carefully applying lessons from our elders and ancestors. We buy the books and devour them like Saturn, consuming the words of the many and applying to that of the one. We honor our deities, our patrons, our gods, the Otherness of it all: we offer the wine and break the bread, we light the flame and burn the fume, we chant the words and walk the path. The road carefully laid before us, we meander in the dark – gifts lain and blood shed – while the branches crackle underfoot or in the fire that we alight. Night. A Crossroads. A frog voices his support and the meadow whispers her sacred truths in the wind. We know our paths, don't we? We know what road we have chosen. Or has it been laid out for us? A

---

[1] Norton, Rosaleen, as quoted by Sonia Bible, 2021. *The Witch of Kings Cross.* Black Jelly Films.

predestined determination from the words of our beloved writers, the charms from our fore-witches, and the niggling voice that asks, "Is this what you have chosen for you? Or is this what you think you should have desired?" The night draws to a close with a staccato of raindrops. Yes, this is tradition. This is for me, you think. Yet, in the devotion are we creating a demolition of our own crafts? Are we loyal to the path, to ourselves, or to those whom we admire? What makes us witches? And, what makes us know? And above all, how to we authenticate while alone?

Practicing my craft from the shadows of the Sierra Nevada mountains, I perch on the foothills, hedge-like and solitary. Traipsing around the vast Californian valley-edges, I forage and make do with the bounty from Earth. In the glory of the Sun I grow and in the majesty of the Moon I burn. Growing, picking, crafting, surrounded by Other, alone. A stack of books inside, yet this is "The Path of the Outcast[2]": unencumbered by fellows, inundated by sources, isolated by continents, uninhibited. Those within cults and covines know the feeling; those in rural Western America or other fringe-like locales epitomize it.

My home boasts the only Mediterranean weather in North America, something that aches of nostalgia for antiquity and magick. Everything grows here, everything is alive. On any given day I may walk with the Forest, bathe with the River, gather collections of ecologically-specific materia unknown elsewhere. I am surrounded by fields of mugwort, chamomile, sage, poppies, mullein, and more, with patches of hemlock and belladonna sprinkled like secrets. The mistletoe embraces the eucalyptus and the moss kisses the stones. The oaks grow tall and the animals leave me dying gifts. I want for nothing. It is in this home I convene with Her and with Him; my oaths sealed in Birch and Blood times over. But the echoes remain – a solitary Californian Traditional Witch: no Appalachia, no Cornish ways, no British and Scandinavian fellows, no archetypal family or rooting history. I will be oaky. Just me, just Them, just the land. Magick.

As I slither through graveyards and stake my home at a three-way intersection, a sensing of Self begins to wash over the façade of aporia[3]. I, too, may sit at the table; I, too, may make rich the Earth of my home that houses no witch-blood through the ages. Whether one is born or initiated (or called), claiming Salem or Essex or Alexandria (or California), a witch is a witch is a witch. We have all experienced a demi-death, and accordingly, life, as Paddon eloquently dubbed, "twice-born." My home knows no deep traditional crafts, save the indigenous rite remnants of the reservations and the missions that mirror not only matriarchal migration, but the concealment of a glaze of whitewash and bourgeoisie. Deep culture, yes, with its own heredities of tradition. But, miasmic[4]. Tainted. Sullied.

2   Paddon, Peter. "The Road Less Travelled." *The Crooked Path Journal,* Issue 2, Summer, 2008.
3   From the Greek "a-" (without) and "poros" (passage), meaning an impasse.
4   From the Greek *miasma,* which translates to "defilement."

So, the establishment of colonization here has blanketed the history, with a bow; the recapitulation of Western America is either regurgitated folklore or appropriated customs for those whose familial roots are not local. There, of course, is the option to apply the traditional paths and "Ways of Old" – from British to Greek to Appalachian to Slavic, the limitless choices abound. But none is me. However, it is easy to embrace Britain's traditional crafts in Britain, no? And that of the Appalachia in the Eastern US, yes? But what of those alone, solitary, isolated... in an area that does not immediately ring a bell of tradition? Is a historical path of cunning for us? For you? For me? We shall carve our names in our own books, wail, burn, and die. We SHALL suffer a witch to live. We shall suffer ourselves.

How does one find their paths in a sea of choices whilst islanded from the regions in which they originated? I have ached to immerse myself in the lands that avow deep histories of the craft; I admire those who write of where they have lived, practiced, experienced. It is simply beautiful. But that has not been my path... nor do I think it ever will be. I love a solid challenge – one that confronts the deepest recesses of my psyche and assaults my ego, scorching in profound and arcane means, illuminating all the areas in which I ache for rawness, growth, and primal lessons. Masochist? Maybe. Eternal seeker? Hell yes. The ever-teeterer on the precipice of æther? I would not have it any other way.

"Twice born," Paddon wrote in this journal, Summer 2008. Thirteen long years and still applicable and relevant as ever. I always thought that meant my denouncement of conditioning and my embracement of craft was new birth, an energetic uterine expulsion of "The Witch." But I was not born just of pacts and paths. I was born of the fire of Self, a guttural moan and crunch of bones within the cosmic reclamation of authenticity, spit like bile at the feet of the Gods. Self is not always beautiful. There is no sterility in one's nature – truth is death, and death is truth. Death is change. Death is growth. And within that death, a fresh foetus ("twice born") emerges: sacred, strong, primordial. A howling with the coyotes. A new ring around a trunk. A phoenix... scorched, ashes, flight. A life, a second life. This, this revival of old within the cawl of Feminine and the starkness of Masculine brings me closer to who I really am. One with Oneness. One with Other. The Earth opens Her belly and devours me whole. Moloch cries. Twice born.

Witchcraft has always been fringe-craft. On the outskirts of society, the edges of towns, the corners of healing, sat the seers and the stirrers and the sorcerers. Acceptance was never acquired. Approval was never ascertained. Scorned and outcast, feared and revered, sought and destroyed, quieted and slayed, we survived in private enigmatic liminality. Witchcraft was never fully accepted, and it was never part of the status quo and cultural norms. Even in antiquity and throughout much of history, the crafts and paths of the Witch was that of the outlying castaways: just a flitter of a shadow in the peripheral, a needed unguent in crisis. Fringe-craft was, and is, the journey of the Self, an insulated cloak of knowing between Us and Them. Witches mark the borders of the fringe obscura. We are the boundaries of all that was and is and will be, via the gifts given, free but not cheap. Sitting in all that is liminal, we wait. We edge.

Once we have acknowledged the liminal fringe-craft within us, we notice a shift: It is then that we are changed. Once touched by Otherness there is no going back. And why would we want to return to the before. "This automatically puts up a barrier between us and mundane folk, which is why we begin to mix only with those who are like us[5]." Of course, this was not this the first time this barrier was noticed, identified, or named (nor will it be the last). Robin Artisson calls this "Witched[6]" – when the Other penetrates and morphs our lives in such a way that we will never be the same. Once we have been Witched, it is difficult to maintain normalcy and redundancy in our day-to-day lives. We know more. We have seen more. We have been transformed forever, and regular friends and customary conversations become tedious. It is not that we do not love these duties; the people and events around us have not changed. We have changed. When surrounded by others who have also been Othered, the transition into being "twice-born" is naturally cohesive. It is not seamless, however, when we are alone or immersed in dullness. It is even more difficult when our solitary nature and distant locations leave us cut off and stranded from the lands of our fore-witches. Nonetheless, we have chosen a rare life; we agreed to the change within ourselves at any cost.

When this change occurs for the solitary, a deep recession into Self commences. There is no doubt of the road ahead, no certainty either. It is then that I reassess all that has been learned. This is for me, I think. This is for me, I know. This devotion is not a demolition of my own craft, even if it differs what I have read or previously applied. There has just been a shift in the loyalty – from that of a pre-carved path to that of my Own. A paradigm of authenticity breaks free, and I know – you know. Where there once sat a stack of books now sits a library of experience. The Knowing. Where there once was a separation of ways is now a relationship with the Wyrd. The Othering. Where there once was a regret of isolation there now is full embrace of Self. The Reclamation. Where there once was doubt and unworthiness there is now an amalgamation of strength. The Witching. And, above all, there is now re-birth. The Twice-Born. It does not matter that my home sits on a hill void of fore-witches and a deep history of tradition. My relationship with Them is all that I need. I gather, I convene, I practice. I am a magician, a sorcerer. I am a Witch. I am magick.

Let us remove the cords of tradition to be re-born into our own Ways. When contact has been made and established with whatever you call all that dwells in the

---

[5] Paddon, Peter. "The Road Less Travelled." *The Crooked Path Journal, Issue 2*, Summer, 2008.
[6] Artisson, Robin. *The Clovenstone Workings: A Manual of Early Modern Witchcraft*, 2020.

Liminality, embrace your Own. Embrace it with that guttural moan, that crunch of bones within the cosmic reclamation of authenticity. Spit your old identity like bile, "twice-born" into Self. Be you Witched or Wyrded, Othered or Owned, it does not matter how much you have read the books or traveled to the places. This is your home. This is your relationship with Them, with You, with the Ways. So, honor you, honor us, honor Them, or die in the fires of expectation and obligation. Emerge reclaimed and real. When you are ready, you may complete this rite:

The Solitary's Sabbat – Connecting and Convening, Us and Them

After initial connection to your own lands and your own ways, you may feel it is time to formally devote, honor, and thank All that has made contact and All that has assisted. This may be after being Othered, after being Witched, but regardless of how or when it happens, you will know you are not the same. You will know you are not alone, even if from the outside you appear completely solitary. At this time you will begin your own cult, your own coven or covine with Them.

> Wander in your area. If you are not in an area that is ripe with natural and open spaces, you may use a park, a tree, a plant in your home – the point is to connect with the Earth, the Spirits therein, and all your own band has to offer and receive. You must not use man-made totems for this rite; you must not use unnatural or un-native plants, icons, or areas. Do some research of the indigenous geni of flora and fauna in your region. Remember, this is your path in your home. The point is to connect and convene, which is not easily done with other species from/or others' practices.

> If you follow the Wheel of the Year, you may choose to perform this rite at Beltane, a traditional time for communion with Nature. It may also be fitting to gauge where the Moon will be, choosing possibly the Dark or New Moon to seal your budding relationships. A waxing crescent or gibbous would also suffice. If you follow a planetary magickal schedule, the days or hours of Jupiter (for responsibility, devotion, honor), Saturn (for discipline, duty, wisdom), or Sun (for knowledge, illumination, patronage, personal power) would be ideal, but really any planetary day or hour could work in your favor depending on the nature of your rite.

> When you have your area chosen, prepare a feast of bread, wine, and whatever else you feel drawn to – this may be milk, eggs, nuts, fruits, etc. Remember to feed the Spirits of your land and leave gifts for anything you may forage. Charm your food, your gifts, and leave them in your area.

Break the bread and share the wine. You may want to light a candle or burn some incense. Follow what your Otherness tells you.

After evocation/invocation/contact, prepare to seal your bond. You may use these words or write your own (including your own deities or spirits):

> Witch Father, Witch Mother, and all in between
>
> Liminal King and Liminal Queen.
>
> Other, Self, Us, and Them
>
> It is here and forever I invite you in.
>
> Formidable, All, the World is yours
>
> I humbly ask for simple honorary tours.
>
> May your bountiful bestowment to my own
>
> Your strength be my own
>
> Your wisdom be my own
>
> Your might be my own
>
> May you shed light on Divine's Secrets
>
> So that I may see.
>
> So that I may help.
>
> So that I may grow.
>
> In your power I claim myself as your Witch.
>
> We share this cord in bread and wine
>
> We connect and convene, for all time.
>
> Thank you, eternally. Thank you.

You may move on to the next rite if you so choose. Thank your Other, your

Spirits, your land. If using flame or fumigant, extinguish. Leave your bread and wine and do not look back.

The Rite of Re-birth and Reclamation – A Witch Wail of Ways

*Prior to the ritual forage and gather the botanic and herbal bounties of your land, but not too much. Save some for the animals, the bees, the Spirits. Be sure to leave offerings of thanks for all that you took.

When the Moon is darkest and your heart is fullest (after you have established your connection to the Spirits of the land around you), leave your residence before twilight and walk towards an area in which you first allied. If the Dark Moon does not work for you, consider using the day or the hour of the Moon. Incorporation of the Moon is of utmost importance, as She signifies transformation, and epitomizes cycles and above all, birth. Furthermore, this being a balance of light and dark, of fire, and of re-birth, Litha or Summer Solstice would work beautifully. When at your place that birthed your solitary personal cult, (which could be a hill, a tree, a lake, a pile of bones, a rock – this is for you to know and you to choose), you may begin. You might and are encouraged to use the same place in which you had your Solitary's Sabbat. This rite is not necessary; it is a way or creating your "twice-born" status after you have been changed eternally by All. It is now in the flames you will be bonded.

Bring your offerings (bread and wine will work) and your foraged plant pieces, light your flame, and commence. If incorporating Litha or Summer Solstice celebrations, the flame or fire may also be jumped over. You may also choose to write on a piece of paper or parchment all that you are no longer, and burn that as well. After invocation, begin.

> Out of the æther You have allowed me to rise.
>
> Your gifts allow me sight through Your eyes.
>
> By tear of blood and crunch of bone
>
> I now reclaim Self for Your own.
>
> I rise again from the flame below
>
> I, reborn, Your Witch aglow.

Doubt, fear, old shame dissipate

Alone, reborn, raw... You recreate.

Out of the primality that endures

I am my Own, but also Yours.

Oh, Witch Mother, how dark your womb!

Oh, Witch Father, how bright flame's bloom!

(Pause, honor your flame. See your death in the flame. Allow the heat of the fires and the coolness of the airs in the Liminality of the gloaming to encapsulate the Light and Dark, the Masculine and Feminine. Use these moments to break yourself from the cords of your past. Sever the etheric umbilical and throw it in the fire – at this time, give your plants, herbs, offerings to the flame.)

In your power I am twice-born as your Witch.

We burn this cord with flame and vine.

We connect and convene, for all time.

Thank you, eternally. Thank you.

Thank your Other, your Spirits, your land. If using flame or fumigant, extinguish. Leave your bread and wine and do not look back.

* * *

Solitary or not, I am never alone. And neither are you. I let the mallow grow wild. I leave the dandelions for the bees. I collect coyote bones and save dead lizards dried on the rocks of the River. I write my own spells, dry my own herbs, make my own oils. I feed the birds. I do not pull the weeds. I clean the rivers and stack rocks around my home. I am forever in my own, MY path, MY cult. But it would not be mine without all that has come before and all that will come to be. The Spirits of this land abound; it does not matter if I am not in the rich deep historical grounds of my fore-witches. I can be the modern version of tradition – my version, Their version – by homogenizing verified praxes with personal gnosis and communion. I am, and forever will be, twice-born in the fires of my Witch Self.

About the Author

The arcane mysteries of the occult allow Lucera occasional passage as Witch, Observer, and Participant. She prefers to work in the kiminal frenzy of Other, her ecstatic escort in writing, reverie, and ritual. Lucera favors her magick as Folk with a Hellenistic Flair, incorporating both tradition and whimsy. She is honored to share her experience and isnpiration by means of word and primal wail.

Which Way Did She Go?

Crowstar

"Which way did she go? Really which way did she go? Wow, she must be a really mighty sorceress!"

"Or just showing off!"

The two women watching her became mesmerized as she disappeared into thin air, followed by a loud AHHH KABOOM!!

"Where did she go?" they asked in unison as they looked around.

As they looked around, they noticed nearby to where they were standing, a patch of earth with a scorched imprint of a broom and star.

"Where do you think she went? What the heck?" exclaimed one of them.

"Look! Up there! There, she is sitting on the moon…That's her leg stretched out over the side of the gibbous edge."

"Mysterious, to say the least." said her friend. "Look, she's leaning back …And there's her head…See it?" said the first woman, still quite mystified by the whole thing.

"And look, there are small stars in her hair…How pretty!"

The other woman then realized something odd and exclaimed partially in horror and partially in disbelief, "I think she's smoking a cigarette!"

"On the moon? That's absolutely sacrilegious!! Blasphemous!! I mean, everybody knows there's no smoking on the moon!"

"Really?" said her friend somewhat doubtfully.

"Yeah, absolutely! They should kick her off!"

"Hey! Watch out for that falling star! It's headed right for us! Quick! Run for your liiiiife!" screamed her friend. They both ran screaming into the night.

"Ha! Ha!" shrieked the great witch.

"Never mess with a witch while she is smoking a cigarette with the Great Lady." added quietly more to herself than anyone else.

"Still, it's a good thing the Lady caught me in time, or I would be flying through the universe, and who knows where I would have ended up? …But that's our secret!… Now, without my broom, how am I going to get down from here? Call the fire department? Ah, I'm so funny."

She was still pondering on a solution when the Great Lady gently picked her up, carefully placed her back down on the earth, and softly whispered, "It's the job of myself and Mother Earth to keep you safe and happy."

The Goddess then gave her a little swat on the rear, and added… "No more drinking and riding!"

The Crooked Path Occult Apothecary

by Raven Womack

Let's do some magick!

Not all *witchy* stores are created equal, nor do they serve their communities in the same way. Some are very goddess-oriented, some are more New Age, some lean more to the spiritual. There are even some that hide in plain sight behind a thin veil of a gift or crystal shop. Then, there are those stores that are full-on, in your face, no doubt about it, let's do some magick kind of shops. **This is The Crooked Path Occult Apothecary!**

The Crooked Path opened its doors in the late summer of 2017, but the spell of its creation had been a long time in the making. Independent shops of all kinds are almost always a reflection of the person or persons whose vision and dreams manifest into an actual shop, but when witches open a store, it's very much like a multi-layered ritual working - constantly unfolding and gaining energy and power.

In a perfect melding of force and form, the Apothecary is the lovechild of Salvatore Santoro and his beautiful wife, Popi. Together they make it happen. Without one or the other, it simply wouldn't work, and those are Sal's words, not mine.

Sal is the force. He's been in and around the magickal community in the Los Angeles area for, shall I say it… decades. Sal was a fixture, an apprentice, an associate, a helper, a student, a teacher, and a million other things in some of the best and most magickal shops in Southern California, but always with his particular East Coast flare. He's also been heavily involved with other alternative cultures and lifestyles (yes, Virginia, to many people, witchcraft is an *alternative* lifestyle). In the years that I've known him, he's managed Goth clubs, trained dominatrixes and submissives, sang in rock bands, and has even dabbled in a few mundane jobs as well. Sal has definitely made a mark in more than one alt-culture arena, but the magick has always been there.

Popi is the form. It's Popi's keen business sense and experience, intelligence, and sharp mind that make it all viable. She is also beautiful, wickedly funny, and has a real sophistication - not that feigned nonsense, so many people try to affect by using big, obscure words. And together, Sal and Popi truly manifested an incredible and magickal space which is also a successful business, and that's not that easy to do.

There's also another woman in Sal's life and the life of the store, and that is the fabulous Scarlett Amaris. Sal describes Scarlett as the beacon and the theologian. While not officially "involved" in the store, Scarlett has been Sal's magickal partner for a number of years, and according to him, she's the only one that can reign him in magickally. She also conducts many of the lectures and classes at the shop, as well as officiating at some of the rituals, and serves as an advisor and confidant.

Even though the shop has only been open a few years, it's already gained quite a bit of attention. Sal, who's pretty much the front man, and the shop have been featured in numerous articles, podcasts, and even on the nationally syndicated radio show Coast-to-Coast with George Noory. They must be doing something right! But it's not the exposure and publicity that makes The Crooked Path a special place. Like moths to a flame, the interviewers and journalists are drawn to the shop's uniqueness and the charisma of the witch, whose personality and magickal philosophy are represented in the shop.

Aesthetics are essential on the West Coast for any kind of shop, and the aesthetics of The Crooked Path are spot on, right down to the black and white checkered floor and the herb garden outside the front door. Oh, and did I mention Beroe, the "inhabited doll" that resides at the store?

If, as a child, you ever looked longingly through the window of a candy or toy shop, you can revisit that feeling by gazing into the front window of The Crooked Path - it's a spell-casters candy shop. When you step inside, you can sense that you're stepping into that "other place" where all things are possible. The Apothecary has all the things that a good witchcraft store should have. Cloaks and cauldrons, crystals and candles, herbs and oils, jewelry and carefully selected books, gris-gris bags and protection jars, statuary and incense, and I'm sure a whole bunch of stuff I haven't mentioned. Like I said… a candy store for witches. But the true focus of The Crooked Path is the apothecary.

The Crooked Path is a true "Occult Apothecary" in every sense of the words. The rows of herbs and oils are not just for show. Sal has created an extensive formulary of original blends of incenses, oils, and potions over the years. He's also very perceptive when it comes to custom formulations, and their prices are extremely reasonable. They also have an herbalist on staff.

One of the things that I noticed right away the first time I was there was the quality and uniqueness of their wares. So many of their products are hand-crafted by small magickal businesses, artisans, and crafters from various backgrounds and traditions. Whether it's Sal, Popi, or one of their employees, they're not only knowledgeable when it comes to their products, but they're also enthusiastic. They simply don't sell anything they don't believe in, and they're happy to give advice or guidance if you need it.

Perhaps one of the most popular features of The Crooked Path is the Candle Bar. *Think salad bar for magickal candles.* There are charts and information available if you need a little inspiration and an assortment of ingredients are available to put together a fantastic spell candle.

Unlike a lot of witchcraft stores, The Crooked Path makes no bones about doing spell work for others. In fact, Sal's services are in great demand. When I asked him if he was concerned about the blowback - because he is definitely not constrained by the Wiccan philosophies and restrictions on the types of spell work he does - he didn't seem at all concerned. As he explained it to me, he is a man with a big collection of hats. When someone engages his services, he puts on the proper hat; when he's done, he takes the hat off and puts it back on the hat rack. Done and done.

Like many of us in the same general age range, Sal came into a witchcraft community that was heavily influenced by the Wiccan movement and the Wiccan take on magical ethics. In his opinion, moral philosophies such as the "Wiccan Rede" and the "The Law of Three-Fold Return" really handicapped many of the aspects of witchcraft and magick. The Golden Dawn and ceremonial magic heavily influence Sal's form and philosophy when it comes to witchcraft; planetary correspondences, flashing colors, and LBRPs are the norm. He loves planetary magick and the simplicity of using planetary powers to craft your workings.

"This is not your grandma's Wicca"

– Salvatore Santoro

Any witch shop worth its black salt, has a community that grows around it. When I asked Sal about the community that has sprung up around their store, he got super excited talking about all the wonderful people that come into the shop and attend the events. He fairly gushed about The Crooked Path community and their openness, diversity, and commitment. It was in large part due to the community's devotion that The Crooked Path made it through the pandemic. The only group that he expressed some frustration with was what he called "The Moldavite Crowd." This is his term for the misguided young wannabe witches who come in to buy moldavite so that they can curse the moon - some crazy thang that started on social media. When I asked him how he handled them, he said he tries to diffuse the situation and correct their misconceptions.

As is often the case, yes… there is a store coven that has manifested through the store, and it has really taken on a life of its own. Sal is crazy proud of them.

I asked Sal, knowing all that he knows, seeing all the hardships and struggles, the traumas and dramas, the feasts and famines that a witchcraft shop deals with, why he decided to open The Crooked Path?

He explained that he wanted to bring practical magick…witchcraft… into the lives of more people. The store is not about spirituality; it's about witchcraft. It's about using roots, herbs, oils, and candles along with the power of the seven ancient planets and using that power to help people break through their limitations.

The Crooked Path also offers classes, rituals, and events, but like everywhere else, the pandemic has really limited the offerings - the safety of his customers and staff is of the utmost importance to Sal and Popi - so many of the classes and lectures moved to an online format. One of the most popular classes is a ten-week series taught by Sal that covers the practicum of witchcraft and culminates with a ritual that is totally facilitated by the students. Scarlett Amaris also facilitates a number of lectures and classes both in the store and online through the store on subjects like, the Wheel of the Year, Hekate and magickal, creative writing.

The Crooked Path has five readers who practice different divination methods and staff with varying specialties and solid general occult knowledge.

The shop hosts many rituals, including sabbats, but perhaps the most important is the annual **Rite of Her Sacred Fires** honoring the patroness of the store Hekate. Their ultimate goal is to create an official Temple of Hekate, and they are well on their way with an incredible temple space. In fact, the temple is Sal's favorite place.

So, if you're ready to do some powerful, hard-core magick, or want to buy some fabulous jewelry or rituals tools or you're just looking to expand your knowledge and you live in the Los Angeles area or you're just visiting Southern California, I would highly recommend checking out The Crooked Path Occult Apothecary. If you can't make it into the shop, be sure to check them out online.

The Crooked Path Occult Apothecary

Location: 2020 W. Magnolia Blvd., Burbank, CA 91506

818-736-5919

walkingthecrookedpath@gmail.com

Website: www.thecrookedpathshop.com

FB: thecrookedpathoccult

IG: thecrookedpath_la

Magick as Dwelling in Truth:

The Unveiling of Alētheia

by Alecto Aletheia Hypatia

I would like to begin with a blessing.

I bless your eyes, that you may see her beauty.

I bless your ears that you may hear her song.

I bless your nose that you may smell her exhilarating bouquet, your mouth that you may taste her delicious fruits, and your lips that you may speak her truths.

I bless your throat that you may always have your own voice, your heart that you may love and be loved, and your mind that you may grow in wisdom, for

Thou art goddess!

A wise woman and witch once told me what I believe to be the secret of magick. It was just a few words, but I have carried this simple saying in my heart ever since.

Every thought a spell, every word a ritual; every word a spell, every act a ritual

I wanted to share these words with you so that we might collectively reflect upon them, imagine what they mean, and visualize their truth.

Reflection

The word "reflect" comes from Latin. It means "to bend back," like a mirror or shiny surface bends light or an image back toward your eyes. A reflection in a mirror will bend your face back as you gaze; a lake will bend back the sky and trees. Mirrored reflections of light glitter and sparkle – each in its own reflective mirror, and together as a scintillating, ever-changing whole.

The mirror metaphor is common. There are many stories about reflections and mirrors. Everyone has heard the story of Snow White and the magic mirror on the wall. Witches use mirrors for introspection - attempts to "look within" and follow the ancient decree of the Delphic Oracle "Know Thyself." Magick mirrors are thus a path to wisdom.

Imagination

To imagine what the words of this saying mean, we reflect upon them. We create an image – a copy, imitation, or likeness. Imagination creates a likeness in our "mind's eye." It is like stamping or casting something – a statuary of the mind.

We can focus on these castings of the mind. When we do this, we bring something home, for the word "focus" comes from the Latin for hearth or fireplace – the heart of the home and family, a place of warmth and nourishment – as a point of convergence or coming together.

Nietzsche says this about knowledge, and his meaning is particularly poignant with regard to the wisdom of the Pythian priestess at Delphi.

We remain unknown to ourselves, we seekers after knowledge, even to ourselves: and with good reason. We have never sought after ourselves – so how should we one day find ourselves? It has rightly been said that: 'Where your treasure is, there will your heart be also'; our treasure is to be found in the beehives of knowledge. As spiritual bees from birth, this is our eternal destination, our hearts are set on one thing only – 'bringing something home'.

– Friedrich Nietzsche, On the Genealogy of Morals

Visualization and the Priority of the Eye

The process of visualization is the work of an artist. Visualizing the truth of words through reflection and imagination renders a creative vision. This creative vision is as much a work of art as is any statue, painting, or melody. All voices, all truths, all reflective imaginations are both singular and collective creative, scintillating, artistic acts.

Have you noticed that these wonderful words: reflection, imagination, and visualization, all refer to the eyes and our sense of sight? We are very sight-oriented. Aristotle thought vision was our most precious sense, but it has also been said that you must become blind to see. When someone loses a sense, other senses will compensate. In what way might our prioritizing of sight blind us?

Our dependence on and prioritization of sight leads us to a kind of distancing and separation from what is seen. In order to see something, it must be separate from us. We see through what, at least to our immediate perception, is empty space. Across the room, I see an object – something over there that is literally "thrown over and against me." Sight implies a duality or multiplicity of others that are separate from me and that I can aloofly observe.

This is objective stance is extremely useful, so much so that it has become our paradigm for knowledge and truth. With the Age of Enlightenment and the dawn of scientific knowledge, it has become the only acceptable basis for knowledge and truth; however, it separates the being of the object observed from the mental reality – that statuary of the mind I mentioned earlier. When working our wills is understood on this model, magic is often construed as "mind over matter." Magick becomes a kind of forceful control of our minds over reality. It looks a lot like our mental will controlling nature, but how can we create reality from a position of objective separation? In what sense could we really connect with reality using this model? There must be another piece to this puzzle.

Fact, Knowledge, Truth

Witches know that objective fact is not the only basis for knowledge and truth. We speak of intuition and of going into the dark. We use various forms of divination, and we cast spells to create or bend reality. In a sense, we are like the mirror that "bends back," but there is more to it.

Other ways of knowing like intuition or dreaming would never be considered knowledge or truth from the objective stance of scientific disinterest. Such a stance is only grounded in the powers of measurement and the verification of visual things; powers that allow agreement among individuals about facts. These powers are based solely on sight; yet how often do we use only the language of the visual, of sight, of the eyes, and of light when talking about what we do as witches? Could there be a problem of language itself at work here? Are we so sight-oriented that our very language has formed itself based on vision? Are our own words boxing us in? We know that it is imperative to be very precise about the words of a spell, but this perspective may lend a new light as to why precision is so important. We use so many metaphors based on sight for knowledge and truth. Does this drive us unknowingly in a particular direction?

Visual Fields of Meaning

I have tried to think of a word that I could substitute for imagination – a word that would mean the same thing but would be based on one of our other senses. I tried to think of the word "image" as if it were based on our sense of smell. I could only come up with the word "bouquet." This was interesting because a bouquet retains the multiplicity of scents while at the same time mixing and melding them together in such a way that the multiple is retained in the harmony of the whole. The sense of smell connects me internally and more directly to the perception in a way that vision does not. The gap between myself and that bouquet of scents disappears because I sense it by taking it inside myself. If I visualize a bouquet of flowers, it is by definition a collection of individual flowers in a bunch together, but there is a difference between the visual bouquet and the smell of a bouquet.

Embodied Magick

A witch realizes that all perception and all experience is synesthetic. It is a combination of all our senses. We never just see a tree, all of our senses are at work – sight, hearing, smell, touch, taste, and maybe even some that are not named here.

We dwell in a synesthetic world. If knowledge and truth are, in some way, based on experience and perception, then in some way, they are no more singular facts than is our dwelling in the world. We are fundamentally involved in the world; we can never absolutely separate ourselves from the world as if it were an external reality cut off from our very being. There is no absolutely objective stance. It is absolute objectivity that is illusory, not the world. Any idea of such absolute objectivity is derivative of our being in the world – of our dwelling at home in the world.

If magick is a way to bend reality through will, then both must be embodied in a synesthetic dwelling in the world with others, both human and other than human beings. Witches recognize that all reality is alive. All that is, lives. Magick is embodied and synesthetic. It brings something home. We change reality only because we are involved or wound up in and with reality as dwellers at home with all that is alive – rocks, mountains, rivers, oceans, air, birds and all other animals, and actions of forging and shaping. From the thoughts we think to the words we utter, to the deeds we do, all is magick. Our thoughts are cast as spells. They are spelled out into reality by our magic alphabets, words, and voices. Our voices and thoughts are rituals of action that shape our deeds, and our deeds, thoughts, words, and voices shape what comes to be in the great tapestry we call reality.

Magick is not "mind over matter." It is our being with and dwelling in the web of being that grounds magick. We can bend reality only because we are intimately involved in reality. We are "Wieirds and Witches" because we bring forth in being and becoming. Whatever is, is what we have wrought. Will is not an isolated mental act that forces itself on the world to change it. Will is embodied and manifests in all that is - even in a flower that seeks the sun. Will is as much corporeal as it is mental, and all beings, whether Earth, Air, Fire, Water, or Spirit, have will rooted in their very being.

Truth as Alētheia (Ancient Greek: ἀλήθεια)

The Greek word for truth is "alētheia." This comes from the word "lēthē" (Ancient Greek: λήθη) and the privative "a" meaning "non" or "un." Lēthē is one of the rivers in the underworld. It is the river of forgetfulness or oblivion from which the dead would drink in order to forget their past lives. Lēthē, therefore, means oblivion in the sense of what is forgotten.

What is forgotten is closed off from us. We no longer have access to what is closed off. We no longer "remember," that is, what is in the river Lēthē is no longer "put together," it is not "re-membered" or "gathered" in any order; instead, it is obliviated. It is relegated to the depths of the womb of Chaos, the endless abyss of darkness and formlessness from which comes all that is.

We cannot see, hear, or smell Lēthē; it is unknowable. Alētheia, therefore, means the un-forgotten, that which is not in oblivion, or that which is not closed off from us. To put this in a positive sense, it is that which is disclosed to us or revealed to us. The truth shows or reveals itself. This disclosure is a constant process. Much like the wheel of the year turns in constant process as an eternal return, so does the process of disclosure roll. This process of disclosure and of becoming is the basis of the word for truth in Greek. Truth is a bringing-out-of-concealment in an evergreen, ongoing process. In mythic terms, it is the weaving of the tapestry of reality, and we are the weavers. It is always this before it can be "seen" as a verification of facts.

Truth as alētheia is much different from our concept of truth today. Our way of understanding truth is based on a correspondence that can be verified. We see truth as verification, not revelation. If what I think matches what is generally perceived in reality, then it is true. If what I say corresponds to what can be verified by accepted methods, then I have spoken the truth. Correspondence and verification do not resemble alētheia; instead, they are derivative of and based upon on this more fundamental idea of revelatory truth.

Our concept of truth today is like a snapshot of a process or a single frame of a movie that can be matched up with something. In fact, that snapshot is part of the greater truth of revelation, but in order to verify for the kind of truth based on correspondence we need a single frame. Trying to verify an ever-changing and flowing process is like trying to put your finger on quicksilver. We need the single picture, the visual separation, and distance in order to verify. The process must be experienced and absorbed, not verified. Only in a freeze-frame can the object that is seen through empty space stand "over there" for you, me, and all who look at it so that it can be verified. But what about the truth as alētheia that produced it? Has the snapshot distorted that truth? Has it only picked out a small piece of the whole and claimed its dominion over all that is real, over all that is knowledge, and over all that can be true?

In all disclosure, there is also that which is not disclosed, for what shows itself in the process of disclosure leaves behind what is not shown; however, the undisclosed is not untruth any more than the great womb of Chaos is untruth. Just because it is not knowable to the eyes does not mean it is untrue. The whole flux, the seen and the unseen, the heard and the unheard, the sensed and the unsensed, is the process of truth as alētheia. What is shown always manifests from the realms of the unknown, from realms of darkness where vision does not dominate all that is. In this sense, intuition is the primordial basis for all knowledge and truth. This is very different from what we typically take for knowledge and truth in today's world.

Language and Spells

Language is itself a creative act. Martin Heidegger made the statement, "Language speaks." This sounds trivial, but when you think of language as only a symbolic representation that allows for communication – a type of verification wherein a truth of one person is transmitted to another – then the creative and transformative discourse that language fundamentally is, begins to show itself. Language first grows out of discourse; what is said creates the path that comes to be formed in language, and all parts of a culture mold the meaning that is transmitted in a language. What gets said creates and forms the language that is spoken on into the future. What is seen only as the most difficult and farthest horizon has no words to speak its name yet—the poet struggles with such distant visions as does the philosopher. Yet, in the speaking, even the vision becomes concretized in such a way that it is distorted, morphed, and changed. How much more difficult is the task when the "vision" is not one of sight but surges up from the depths of the unseen, from the womb of Chaos? Is this perhaps the more primordial basis for carefully wording our spells and carefully ordering our thoughts before we speak them forth?

Magical Paradigms of Mystery

The procedural and revelatory truth of non-oblivion and the creative act of language fit well with paradigms of magick and witchcraft. The wheel of the year, the changing nature of the world, the mythic themes of weaving reality, and descent into darkness and the underworld, both realms of the unseen and the shapeless, and intuition are all specifically non-objective ways of experiencing reality, gaining knowledge, and of finding truth. The creative act of language is how we speak this forth into reality – we cast spells, we literally spell it out. Derivative, objective knowledge is thus, in a sense, illusory, not intuition, since intuition is closer to the generating source cloaked in the depths of an underworld where the sense of vision does not work well. Maya's veil does not cover and hide reality, making all that we see in this beautiful world an illusion; it is the mysterious source of reality itself.

Reprise

So, what is revealed in the words spoken by my wise witch friend? How must we approach this saying that I have carried with me ever since she whispered the secret to me? I can only begin the conversation. The words merit and deserve a diversity of reflections, imaginations, and truths. They need to scintillate. They also demand our synesthetic attention. They demand the dark and the shapeless realms. Hades is literally the shapeless one. Persephone is the thrasher and so the destroyer of the corn. She breaks the cob into its kernels or fragments. She destroys the image so we may artistically recreate her beauty and truths. Dwell with these words. Penetrate them. Enter into the dark. Reflect upon them. Become artists of destiny and truth.

The goddess is one, yet she is the goddess of 10,000 names. May your truths be beautiful works of art, and may we all be blessed with the diverse beauty we create as we dwell together in truth.

I bless you, and I bless that you are, for you are all goddess.

For the secret, I thank Live Oak Womon.

For the philosophical guidance, I thank Friedrich Nietzsche and Martin Heidegger.

For the desire and yearning, I thank the maiden, mother, and crone in all her names.

Blessed Be!

About the Author

Alecto Aletheia Hypatia has a BA and an MA in Philosophy as well as a BA in French. She has been a witch for over 35 years and an elder priestess in the Dianic tradition for over 30 years. She has taught Philosophy for more than 25 years.

You can not blindfold a man and expect him to carry you across the river.

African Proverb

The Gods Are Not Your New Toys

Cultural Demonization and Cultural Appropriation

by Mark NeCamp

I did not realize I was black until 3rd grade. I had no idea what this thing called race was. I just assumed people had different skin color, like they had different colored eyes, and that was just the way it was. In 3rd grade, people asked me "what I was" and I did not know how to answer them. After a particularly painful day of school yard bullying, my mother explained to me what "black" and "white" were and that I was both. It would take me another twenty plus years to come full circle on what race meant to me, and how I reconciled the different branches of my heritage by adopting a global perspective.

Demonization of African Culture & Religion

My mother was very active in African-American culture and movements. I went to fundraisers with the family of slain Black Panther, Fred Hampton. I met the mother of Emmett Till, and heard her pride and pain. For me being "black" was a matter of pride and strength. I remember when I was 5 years old and I went to the local library for books. I remember the bright red and patterned cover of a book of stories I loved: Anansi the Spider. I loved how clever he was, and laughed at the trouble he got in to. So why did it take me until my twenties to look at the Gods of Africa as sources for inspiration?

My mother had raised me on a steady diet of horror movies, and supernatural thrillers. My grandmother had prophetic dreams, and always dreamed of fish when someone she knew was pregnant. I went to a Catholic church where more than a handful of the parishioners wore elekes, the necklaces of practitioners in the religions derived from the worship of the orishas, the ancestor/spirit/deities of the Yoruban people of Africa. I lived about a mile from the largest Hoodoo shop in Chicago, Lama Temple, which was situated right off that major thoroughfare and ley line called the Dan Ryan Expressway. My first magical teacher was an old African-American man named Goldfinger. He wore the sort of uniform that a mechanic might wear, with his name on an embroidered white patch with red lettering, and had a warm, beaming smile, highlighted with a golden tooth. This was near the end of high school, and I was far more intrigued with the mystery of what I learned to even think about using it for a love spell to get a girlfriend, or even get revenge on some of the kids that bullied me. I was content to be privy to a mysterious world that I was able to escape to and made me feel better about myself the more my knowledge grew. Why did I learn so much about Hoodoo, but not about its cousin religion of Vodou?

The answer to some of these questions is a complex one. It is apparent that African-American culture has had many changes and leaders. Leaders such as Marcus Garvey helped paint a picture of an idealized African motherland that black people could feel a part of in spirit. Heroes such as Dr. King and Malcolm X opened the way to dialogues and movements that permanently changed the face of African-American society; and grassroots organizers such as Jesse Jackson tried to reinvigorate and mobilize African-Americans to empower themselves through community service and political action. All of these people have fought against one of the most devastating and subtle enemies to all African-Americans: internalized cultural demonization.

When slaves first came to America, it was not enough to enslave them, rape them, treat them like cattle, and murder dignity; there was also the destruction of their indigenous culture. Slave owners actively worked to destroy African religion as a method of control. There was no way to overtly transmit stories or ritual, when the Gods of Africa became "demons" in the eyes of slave owners. While religion was more than likely beaten out of people, it follows that the demonization of African deities became internalized in nascent African-American culture so that any indigenous African religion was seen as either "superstition" or "devil worship".

Some clever groups of people were able to syncretize their Gods with the Christian religion they were forced to follow- becoming the religions of Ifa, Lacumi, Candomble, Santería, and others.

Today, most African-Americans- about 83%- are Christian. Polytheism to the modern African-American is something that is comparably rare. The mythology of Africa is usually seen as something to be studied under the auspices of African studies, folk literature, and cultural anthropology.

How Cultural Appropriation Reinforces Demonization

Around the same time I was learning about Hoodoo, I was doing a lot of Buddhist meditations, reading New Age books such as *The Celestine Prophecy* and going to the Hare Krishna temple, at the advice of one of my best friends. From my time with the Hare Krishna devotees, I learned about polytheism, Hinduism, and the importance of devotion in spirituality. Although the Hare Krishnas are henotheists that worship Krishna, one of the most popular incarnations of Vishnu, I strangely came away with a love of Ganesh.

By the time I went to college, I was a strange Hindu-Hoodoo-Buddhist with an interest in Shamanism. I had not really heard of Paganism until I found work at a local incense shop, which happened to actually be a Pagan store. The manager of the store became my first high priestess, and I generally respected her, until one day she announced she had been learning about the religion of Ifa, and announced our coven would be learning about the orishas. Our priestess dutifully informed us which orisha "ruled our head" and that I "was a Chango". What this meant to me was that because I was the most masculine member of our group, I was supposed to worship the Spirit of Thunder, Masculinity, Kingship, and Warriors because that was the image that she chose to project upon me. This was a disaster! I was having my sense of masculinity defined by someone, at a time I was struggling with those same issues. To make things worse, I felt like I was expected to live up to the stereotype of "black man as sexual conqueror" and eventually I was kicked out of the coven for not being aggressive enough, or engaging in a relationship with her. Obviously, trying to put me in this sort of category was also a subtle form of racism in the sense I would fit a specific stereotype.

My self-image for myself did not include me as a "stud", but I can honestly say it did contribute to issues I had later with having an unhealthy relationship with my sexuality, self-loathing, and confusion to who I was. I think this is something that happens to a lot of people of color when figuring out who they are and how that relates to their personal religion. Disconnection from the dominant culture, internalized cultural demonization and stereotypes, and lack of support from African-American culture for African polytheism creates a chaotic environment to find an authentic sense of self and relationship with the Gods. The only way I can address this in my personal life through ancestor worship, re-connection with the African deities, and mindfulness of the situation.

How Pagan Theology Can Inspire Cultural Appropriation

Paganism is not just a religion, or even a group of religions- it is a culture. The problem with and utterly beautiful virtue of it, is that Paganism as a culture is composed of individuals that for the most part are expatriates or co-citizens of at least another culture. We have everything from hippies, to goths, ex-Catholics, ex-Fundamental Christians, feminists, academics, poets, you name it. It is the most amazing mixture of unique individuals that anyone could imagine (unless you lived in Manhattan, probably). There is no ultimate definition or any theology that could be considered orthodox- instead there are trends and popular beliefs. One popular aspect of modern Pagan theology that has assisted in cultural appropriation is soft polytheism.

Soft polytheism is the belief that the Gods- be they Zeus, Kali, Hecate, Hermes, etc.- are manifestations of the Universe. They could be thought of as different masks that "God" puts on. A variation of this belief is duotheism, where there is one God and one Goddess, with all Gods being a manifestation of the God, and all Goddesses being an aspect of the Goddess. The latter belief is more popular in Wiccan theology. Soft polytheism contrasts directly with hard polytheism: the belief that all deities are completely separate. There are many schools of thought that range from one end to the other on the debate between "soft" and "hard", but that is the basis of a different article. If all deities are One deity, in a duotheistic model, then by transitive property my worship of Zeus can be equated with Shango. Both are Gods of thunder and kingship, and if all Gods are the God, then there should not be a problem right?

The problem is that this undermines the value of both the cultures of the ancient Greeks and Africans at the same time. A cultural bleaching is occurring where the subtleties and histories of entire civilizations are lost. I think it would be a similar way of saying "since all men are equal, I am going to equate the experience of a man from Greece, to one in Nigeria". In this case, the spirit of equality generalizes complex motifs into something that destroys the cultural, spiritual, and emotional impact of the things it seeks to celebrate. To be fair, an extreme of hard polytheism can create cultural biases that can feed prejudice, intolerance, and racism. Many reconstructionist movements are hard polytheists by nature and seek to go back to not only worship of the Old Gods. The danger is that this tribal identity based on the reconstructionist culture supersedes other cultural memberships and can lead to cultural superiority.

Inspiration from the Gods versus Cultural Theft

When Diana Paxson, the mother of the modern Heathen movement, was trying to understand some of the lost religious practices of the Norse, she looked at a very unlikely source- Voodou. In Norse traditions, there is a practice called seidr. This is a type of ritual where a celebrant is seated in a place of reverence and they are expected to be ritualistically possessed by a deity, where the purposes for this range from information about problems that plague the tribe, to communion with the God that you are spiritually connected to. The rituals and specific shamanistic like spiritual technology that has been used to get to the ecstatic states of consciousness needed for the possession work had been lost to time. Knowing that Vodou is a religion that centers on possession work, Paxson was able to analyze and deconstruct those techniques, and use that knowledge to reconstruct the Norse equivalent. Diana Paxson was inspired by another's religious practice, but did not seek to copy it for her own practice that supplanted or disavowed the cultural context from whence it came.

Modern Paganism is an eclectic movement, for an eclectic time. I have heard many Pagans describe their spiritual practices along the lines of following a hybrid path of "Buddhist-Pagan" or "Christo-Pagan". I've also heard people naming a list of all of the different things that they practice, and where they came from. I do not think this is cultural theft. I think the line is crossed when ignorance breeds a fetishism of another spirituality and culture (i.e. the fetishism of Voodou as the "cool new thing"), or when someone attempts to partake of that culture in an inauthentic manner. Recently I had a conversation with Ian Corrigan, from Ár nDraíocht Féin (ADF), which is a Druidic organization that allows membership to anyone following spirituality within the Indo-European cultural umbrella. Ian has been with ADF for a number of years and is one of the most esteemed elders of that group. I asked him why the deities and culture of the African Diaspora was not something that ADF worked with, since there were many similarities between the traditional Indo-European cultures and the African ones. He told me that it was something that was discussed at one point, but that "no one felt it was right to 'reconstruct' something that already had a culture".

Pan-Global Pantheons and the Road to Authentic Eclecticism

For my personal spiritual journey, I have been doing work researching and working with the deities of the Akan people of Western Africa. Akan means "first", as in they are the first people of Africa. I have found resonance with how their main deity is a panentheistic one, that is the unknowable source of all origins, with many other polytheistic deities of the earth, healing, war, etc. I am purposely working with a pantheon that has not been exploited the way the other religions of the African diaspora have. I have seen too many people trying to take advantage of people financially, and otherwise, in the name of initiating someone into a tradition. I am trying to develop a spiritual root that hearkens to and heals the spiritual wound I have from being divorced from a continuous spiritual line that directly stretches from the ancestors I know back to Africa. I am also re-working my ancestor worship since that is something common to most Pagan paths and helps me connect with my roots on a visceral and personal level.

I believe we are in a place where we are becoming part of a larger global culture. I feel that the relationships we have with the Gods, and that they have with us, are similar to what we would have with any individuals and that as long as we are trying to be respectful, our insults will be forgiven the way a parent, friend, or partner forgives honest mistakes. To progress forward as a species, we must build our collective lives on principles of unity and a compassion that speaks to that unity. This does not mean that I think I have the right answer, or that any of the multitude of ethnic reconstructionist groups do either; it means that we need to have dialogue. I think the safest rules are simple (but not easy): if someone is offended by what you are doing, then take a moment to reflect if you are committing cultural appropriation; if you feel shame for investigating the Gods of your Ancestors, then question why; and if you are inspired by a certain religious practice, analyze or integrate it into your own spirituality without insult or injury to that culture.

Bibliography

"The Black Church." *BlackDemographicscom*. <http://blackdemographics.com/culture/religion/>.

Merry, Sally Engle, "Human Rights Law and the Demonization of Culture (And Anthropology Along the Way)" 2003. Polar: Political and Legal Anthropology Review 26:1: 55-77.

Paxson, Diana L. Essential Asatru: Walking the Path of Norse Paganism. New York: Citadel, 2007.

Young, Jason. "The Journal of Southern Religion 14 (2012)." *The Journal of Southern Religion · African Religions in the Early South*. <http://jsr.fsu.edu/issues/vol14/young.html>.

About the Author

Mark NeCamp is a tarot reader, healer, writer, teacher, spiritual alchemist, modern day practitioner of the Art, and a devoted family man. He teaches classes using magic as a tool for personal growth. He is passionate for how we each can, through the alchemical process, turn our spiritual lead into gold as individuals and as a global tribe. He has led many community groups in the Midwest, and currently sits on the Board of Directors for Wolf Run Wildlife and Spiritual Sanctuary located in Remus, Michigan. He can be found at blackstagalchemy.com.

ON THE MAKING OF MAGICAL TOOLS

by John E. Breen

I am a maker. I make things. Even as a little kid, my favorite thing to do was to make things. I always thought it was just me and my family or our circle of friends. My father was a maker, as was his father before him. There were even family stories of a time during WWII when my grandfather and some friends gathered discarded items and built toys for the neighborhood kids so Santa could still make his rounds. My mother's family had farmed through the great depression, and that experience left its mark. Mom was the mistress of making clothes work and re-work, altering and reshaping garments to make them get just a bit more use. The kitchen was her temple and her workshop. She read cookbooks like other people read novels. No one ever left her table hungry, and she knew how to stretch a meal. So when I was growing up, making things was just something that we did. Oh, we bought plenty of things, but it was always the things we made ourselves that gave us the most satisfaction.

I came into the study of Paganism and witchcraft in the mid-1980s. At that time in Southern California, a few shops carried the tools or things needed to create a Pagan practice, but not many, and the age of the internet and online retail was still decades away. There were mail-order catalogs. However, as with all things one sends away for, even today: "you pays your money, and you takes your chances!" What was an up-and-coming student of the craft to do? Especially when there was not a lot of spare money in the budget of a college student embarking on this new and exciting path that, quite frankly, had some wicked cool gear!

Luckily for me, it was the mid-1980s! While much of the world was swept up in a wave of mass consumerism that looked like the last days of Rome, the generation of writers on Wicca, witchcraft, and the occult at that time and the generation before them had a very DIY spirit. Perhaps it was because, like my family, they had come through several big wars and economic depressions, and therefore had a mantra of "make do and mend." Maybe it was because there were so few resources to acquire tools of the craft in those days and if you wanted a thing, you HAD to make it.

The first book I had (like so very many of my generation) was *Buckland's Complete Book of Witchcraft* by Raymond Buckland. In it, he gives instructions for making some of the things you would need to practice Wicca and when I read this, I knew I was where I belonged. Many people talk about the feeling of "coming home" when they relate how they first heard that the craft embraced a female deity or had a closer tie to the natural world. For me, it was reading about how I got to make the things I would be using to practice the craft! Buckland, and other writers I was reading voraciously at the time, like Doreen Valiente and Scott Cunningham, expressed the idea that by making a ritual tool yourself or at least changing a purchased item it is some way, such as decorating it, you were adding your essence to it and imbuing it with power that could be tapped into later.

So I started making Pagan and Wiccan stuff. Because of my background, it came fairly easy, though there were failures! Mistakes are inevitable, and I made some good ones! Some required redesigning, and some required medical attention, but each mistake taught me lessons that I still carry with me. Over time friends asked me to make items for them, and then I started making items for sale to small retail shops. As a matter of fact, I still do. Every so often, I will get a message from a retailer in my area, and then it's "call up the troops, all hands on deck, we need to get a dozen brooms made!" These get to be teaching days, future makers get taught, and a shop gets some handcrafted stock; everybody wins! Sometimes it is just one item, and the person who wants it is in no particular hurry. Those are great projects because I get to spend a bit more time on them and make a piece that I really feel good about. All the "production" items are made with care and attention to detail, but it's the single "One-Offs" where I genuinely take my pleasure. I know I will never get rich making ritual items, but it fills a place in my soul like nothing else does.

We live in an amazing time (though I imagine every generation could say that). With access to online retailers, it is much easier to find the things we need for our Pagan practice. Even a quick internet search will yield results that range from one-of-kind, handcrafted items that are worth every penny (don't get me started on "hagglers") to a place I found called "Pagan Stuff Cheap," and the name is pretty much accurate. The rise of online retail has attributed to the demise of many brick and mortar shops. But it has also proven a boon to the individual craftsman who now has a much broader audience for their wares. The former is a true shame because regional shops have their own style, and the items they stock often reflect this, but I can't argue with the benefit of the latter for both the maker and the buyer.

Along with those internet-related things mentioned before, the rise of "maker culture" has been incredible! When I found out, there were others out there who, like myself, also MAKE STUFF and that there are groups, meetings, and events where people gather to share information and techniques; it was that homecoming feeling from my early days as a new Pagan all over again.

"There are two rules on the spiritual path...being and continue."

-Old Sufi Saying

The Philosophy and Magic Behind Crafting

To my way of thinking, there is a philosophical side to making things that will be used for magical purposes. The entire process of making the item becomes a part of the energy of that item. When we learn, we improve our overall knowledge and make the totality of existence better. In Jungian psychology, there is the idea of the collective unconscious, a body of knowledge that is shared between the minds of human beings without the need for direct transmission. In other words, we all just know things. Some anthropologists think this knowledge was more accessible to early hominids. Many current tribal cultures speak of "memories" that are shared by members; in many ways having access to those memories shows membership in that culture, whether a person was born to it or not.

But, before we tap into the infinite "maker mind," we want to make sure we are prepared to act on the knowledge we are tapping into, so, when I am about to begin a project, I try to make sure of the following things:

Research

Have I one my research? I want to make sure I know as much as possible about the material(s) I will be working with and how they behave. You can't account for every variable, and learning from the material itself is part of the enjoyment. When working with new material, it's a good idea to know if what you are working with is going to give you the result you are looking for or not.

Study the techniques you will be using as well. If possible, watch some videos of people making the kind of thing you are working on or using the type of construction method you will be using. You can avoid a lot of mistakes that way or at least have a good jumping-off point. Over time, you will develop your own style of doing things, but it's good to have a solid foundation. You will develop your own style of doing things over time, which is good for the time being though you will have a solid foundation. If there are no video or written resources on a technique, that's okay too; you get to be a trailblazer.

Try things out. Do a practice piece. If something doesn't work, and you tried the way you found it in your research, then find your own way to achieve the goal.

Nature, Appearance, and Feel

Part of your research will be to decide and discover the magical item's nature and how it will look and feel. Sometimes this requires inner reflection to gain insight. Part of what makes these items unique is the energies they carry. By understanding the energies of the ritual item you are creating, you can add to those energies as you make it. By tuning into these energies and working with them, we can make more effective ritual items. I am not saying that if you don't feel the connection that you shouldn't go ahead with the project, you may gain that connection through the process of construction. It is, however, really nice if you can go in with that door open to you already. So spend some time with the material and get to know its nature, how it speaks to you and how you speak to it. A relationship of mutual respect and understanding can really enhance your overall experience on a project.

As a part of your preparation, take a look at the magical nature of the materials you select for the project. Different materials, shapes, and colors have various magical correspondences. For example, the color gold and gold-colored metals such as brass have cultural and historical association with the sun and its power. So you would not use it as the primary material in a moon goddess talisman, for instance? Most goddesses in western esoteric traditions are associated with the moon and colors like blue and silver.

However, these correspondences come from several sources and don't always agree. Case in point, in the above example, a number of cultures see the moon as masculine and the sun as feminine. For them, a brass goddess talisman would be entirely in line with their cultural experience. So, use the materials that resonate with you or for the person you are creating the item for, as this will be important when the ritual object you are making is used. Some of the projects will have one material, and some will have many.

There was an interesting discussion on Cory and Laine's New World Witchery podcast on the nature of magical items. Are they innately magical because of what they are made of? Are they magical because the materials react to each other to create the magical energy (like a chemical reaction)? Or do magical items need to be "charged" or "activated" to be effective? In my personal opinion, it is a bit from all of them. I think the materials have energies that are innate to them and by bringing them together in certain ways the energies can be enhanced and directed. By "charging" or "activating" the ritual item, a link is created between the user and the tool. This link becomes a conduit to the energies of the tool to you and you to it. The act of charging the item focuses those energies that are contained in the tool. We will address a method for this process of charging a bit later.

Gather What is Required

Make sure to review the process for your project. Gather all the tools and materials you think you will need before you start. It's much easier to have all the things you need right to hand if possible. Since this is "creation as meditation," it is better if you don't need to break your flow to go and get something. So, read twice, cuss less! If you do have to stop and fetch something, just take it in stride. Creating magical tools is a magical process and negative emotions can impede that.

Prepare Your Space

In my experience, there are generally two kinds of craftsmen, those who require a neat and tidy space and those who don't. The ones who like it neat seem to find that clutter is a distraction and keeps them from focusing on the task at hand. Others prefer to be surrounded by bits and pieces or projects and materials and find inspiration in the midst of the "chaos." Whether you are in one camp or the other or somewhere in-between, spend some time before you begin a project to prepare the place you will be working. This goes hand-in-glove with the next item.

Prepare Yourself

The project you are making is not a strictly utilitarian item and by preparing your workspace (and that includes your inner workspace), you set this time and this work aside as special. Your mental and emotional state will have great influence on the energy or the item you are making. So, take a moment, look around and appreciate that you are doing something unique. Something that connects you to the gods, ancestors, and spirits as well as to all those that have gone before who have crafted items for the altar. I like to take a moment before I begin to recognize this and I find it really helps me. I can feel those who have gone before looking over my shoulder and giving advice. If the time and space allow, I will often light a candle before I start and share a drink of water or ale with them to strengthen this connection. You might also use a prayer or mantra for this time.

Prayer Before You Begin

As I stand in this place of creation,

May my spirit be joined with the spark of inspiration,

May creativity flow though me,

May it wash over me,

May it bear me along in the great current of making,

This place is special,

This time is special,

May my work be blessed.

Time Allotment

Sufficient time allotment is always one of the hardest things for me to do. I am notorious for not allowing myself enough time. This can result in stress that will influence the energies in the item you are making. Always keep what I refer to as your "time budget" in mind. If your crafting is getting in the way of other things, re-evaluate. Should those other things be taking priority? This is a decision that only you can make.

Countless times I have had to forgo sleep, food, and other work to meet a deadline. It would have been better if I had budgeted my time more closely. This is the lesson I have learned and now I give it to you. In the end, this is a choice you are making. Don't blame others for how you opted to spend your time. Accept that it is a choice you made and that you could have chosen differently but did not. Learn from this and when the next time comes, you will get to make this choice again. Do not begrudge. The time I spend crafting is some of the best moments of my life. When I see the finished item and think of the process of its making, I know that this is the work that I am called to, and as such, I want to make sure that it is the best I can make it.

Conclusion

Over the years, I have derived a great deal of pleasure and satisfaction from making ritual tools for others as well as myself. I hope that this brief look at my process and philosophy helps your work on your next project. Be guided by your Gods and Spirits, approach the task with reverence and joy, take your time and enjoy the journey. Take notes! Help others!

Endnotes

https://newworldwitchery.com/resources/podcasts/

About the Author

John Breen has been a practicing Witch for over 30 years. A lifelong crafter and maker of things, John especially enjoys making items for use in ritual and spiritual practice. He owns his own business, Hexenhaus, selling handcrafted and carefully curated items at www.hexenhausshop.com, which can also be found on Facebook and Instagram.

John is married and has two amazing daughters. He lives in Oregon.

A Poem by J.P. Sedgewick

A stately Yew resembles Fir
On Gorse choked distant height
Until the mounts of Heather
End age and vexsome flight.
Idho-yew, then silver Fir
Join life's return to Birch.
O glain of sard, O Willow white
Begin I on eon's search.

Birch was the whip with
Lightning from the mime,
Nascent in Her splendor
Forgotten is his crime.

Saille and the Moon is She
He dared not meet Her at the door.
Denied he Her as lithe maid of tree,
Then
Caught he winking Hazel eye from shore.

Made to drink of Ivy mead
Given bitter berry wine and crown of Gorse,
Prisoned these long years yet newly freed
Reluctant rides She on elder horse.

Birch was the stinging whip,
Saille Moon
Turn on 'til eon's end.
Coll's wondrous wisdom hails
Deliverance from recent trend.
Quert and Willow no longer fey,
Fearn, not felled, has Her alban bough in sway.

J. P. Sedgwick ~ Bard Amergin

About the Author J.P. Sedgewick

"My father came to the goddess late in life. I had given him a copy of The White Goddess by Robert Graves. He poured over it. He claimed the name of bard and wrote a poem dedicated to the return of the goddess. Unfortunately, he did not walk on Earth's meadows long after that, but he told me that the book had answered questions that had puzzled him all his life and that he now would dedicate himself to the goddess. This is his poem. He was taken to Avalon in 1988. I know he is now an inspiration for all poets who listen to the mists and pluck silver and gold apples. I am thrilled to finally, at long last, have his loving tribute to the Lady published."

– Emily Sedgwick

Paganism, Diversity, and the Pandemic

By Kelsey Pullaro

For those new to the path, the sheer vastness of the history of Paganism can seem daunting. In its simplest form, Paganism is the worship of the Earth and its mysteries. Therefore, the exorbitant amount of diversity within the Pagan community largely stems from the centuries of nature-worshipping subcultures unifying in their most basic principles and practices. This duality of diversity and unity is somewhat unique to the Pagan community, and is perhaps what has allowed the tenets of Paganism to prosper throughout history.

Growing up within the deeply patriarchal Christian church, the limited spiritual history that I had access to was so obviously not designed with anyone like me in mind, I never felt connected to my religion or that I possessed any actual spirituality of my own. I often felt purposefully excluded from the most sacred practices of the religion I was born into simply because I had the projected misfortune to be born female. As I grew, so did my contempt for Christianity, and I pushed back against the puritanical society of the Baptist community around me with every conscious decision of my identity. For decades I built myself around the rejection of anything religious, spiritual, or sacred. My formative years taught me that there was no great deity in the sky judging my every thought and action, and led me to the conviction that if, by some miracle there was a God in heaven, that I rightfully stand in judgement of him. For decades I operated with the intention to close myself off from anything I could not identify with my five senses. Then, I began to learn about Paganism.

As an adult, being introduced to another way of life elicited a complicated emotional response. The radical rejection of the spiritual practices of my youth converged with the current sociopolitical strife and global pandemic in a perfect storm of deep-seated need. A need for acceptance, representation, and respect that I had never received from the rigid social structures I came from. Through the fear and uncertainty of multiple quarantines, losing loved ones to the denial of basic human rights (and not the deadly virus ravaging the world around me), and the sudden confrontation of self and perceived self, I stumbled upon another world that seemed to be waiting for me. Paganism holds space for the marginalized and the minority celebrates individuality, and honors the many different paths its practitioners choose to take.

Modern-day Paganism encompasses a multitude of religious and cultural beliefs that have been characterized as 'other' in the dominant Judeo-Christian culture of the modern era; and while the etymology of the word Pagan is geographically rooted in ancient Greece and Rome, the term and its broad practices have always referred to beliefs outside of Christianity. Perhaps the most inclusive aspect of modern Paganism is its acceptance of Humanist, agnostic, and atheist practitioners. Because the central most tenet of Paganism is simply that the divine lives within nature, the acceptance of one or more deities is not necessary to a fulfilling spiritual existence.

When the pandemic swept across the country last year, I began offering virtual tarot readings to my small social media community and learned that while we each have our own individual issues, the root of our problems was the same; we all felt directionless and as though the meaning had been stripped from our daily lives. These readings became a kind of therapy, and provided a unique sense of empowerment through intuition. Experiencing the diversity of individuals within the Pagan community firsthand during the pandemic led me to the discovery of an inclusive community to process collective and individual trauma, which proved invaluable during a time of global uncertainty.

During each reading, a connection was made, not only for my clients and their cosmic questions, but between the client and me and our shared hardships and fears during what was the most difficult period in our lives. The space that was held for these intimate interactions with complete strangers during a time of such intense isolation was made possible because of the diversity and inclusivity in Paganism. The willingness to share common beliefs and practices while also maintaining and validating the importance of different paths and beliefs is the mechanism that allows Paganism to continue to be accessible to those seeking a spiritual community outside of the Christian norm.

It is not entirely uncommon for a modern spirituality practice to be inclusive; however, what sets modern Paganism apart is that it has consistently been more inclusive than Judeo-Christian culture. Modern Paganism has long been a haven to those who feel marginalized and oppressed by the Christian church. Paganism's openness to difference has nurtured a dedication to the honoring of spiritual practices across cultures within its spiritual practitioners. The adoption of early Hellenic traditions by the Romans and their subsequent integration into the daily lives of the general population illustrates the principle for this propagation of belief systems that have since been replicated throughout modern history.

Perhaps the most transcendental rituals across cultures are those dealing in divination. These rituals and their history have been exchanged time and again in what I believe is an effort to provide similar community and connection to those who exist outside of the sociocultural norms of their time and place. The additional effort to provide cosmic explanations for variables beyond current comprehension can be viewed as an optional bonus to those who seek and find spiritual comfort in the Pagan community.

The broad community of Paganism wouldn't be what it is without those dedicated to the preservation of their chosen deities, rituals, and practices. However, their willingness to teach these incredibly personal soothing techniques without the expectation of a complete alignment of beliefs indicates that a belief system uncontrolled by patriarchal society breeds a willingness to coexist rather than to conquer.

As someone who identifies as atheist, my ability to find moments of spiritual community in a time of global crisis and great emotional need speaks to the spirit of inclusivity present within the Pagan community. The diverse cultural representation that has always been central to modern Paganism continues to be represented through the practitioners who pass down rituals and their meanings in an effort to bring comfort to others without the expectation of reciprocation, and their efforts continue to bring comfort to those living outside of Christianity.

About the Author

Kelsey Pullaro is a wife, mom, tarot and rune reader. She lives in the mountains and has a BA in Creative Writing and English.

A Witch Among The Herbs

*Materia Magicka
of Herbs, Flowers, and Trees*

Spells

Craftings and More

Ilana Sturm

To Kindle the Magickal Flame

Excerpt from: A Witch Among the Herbs

(Pendraig Publishing 2016)

by Ilana Sturm

I can remember clearly the moment that would set me on a path apart from the everyday world; The Crooked Path! It was a Tuesday in September, around midday, and I had accompanied my mother on an errand to pick up some special herbs from the three old ladies that lived on the corner block in an old ramshackle house with an overgrown garden.

I was about eight years old. It was 1969, and a man had just walked on the moon. People were striving to find themselves, and for the first time ever, different paths and different ideas were coming to the fore. Remember, this was Australia; we experienced the 60's about ten years after everyone else in the world.

Now my family could never be considered your 'average' family unit. We weren't Travellers, but we lived like them, constantly on the move, living off our wits. My mother would rather have died a hundred deaths than visit a doctor for anything and made sure she always had a well-stocked herb pantry for the small ailments that came our way. As a child growing up in a transient existence, no steady income, no home, and very few possessions should have been something of a harrowing experience, but I can honestly say, although we had no worldly goods, we were loved and cared for. In our house, we practiced herbal healing, astral travel, and psychokinetic ability.

One of my favourite games was trying to place a thought in another family member's mind to have them say or do a certain thing, and my father and I would sit for ages concentrating our thoughts on the task at hand. My mother read palms; she had a real knack for it, and I can remember the people coming to whatever house we were renting with looks like startled rabbits; half excited and half scared of what they might be told.

My mother was a kind and positive person; I think she helped a lot of souls, most of whom were scared of their own shadows and who probably thought we were – well, I'm not sure what they thought we were. Certainly, we never used the word witch or magic, but I guess it was always there, hanging in the air. My grandmother, who died when I was only 12 years old, was to me a bit of a mean old woman. Although she'd had seven children of her own, I don't think she liked children at all. She certainly had no time for them or me.

The only good memories I have of her were seeing her in the garden growing her beloved herbs or in the kitchen. Oh my, that woman could cook! Then, of course, there was her fabulous Book of Secrets. I got to look in it (look, but never touch) whenever she took it out to make up any kind of formula or potion for whatever ailed us.

We were of Jewish heritage, but my grandmother was pure Celt. She had a broad Scottish accent, although her people were originally from Ireland. Born on the ship taking her mother and father from Ireland to Scotland, she had all of the Celtic fire within her and luckily for us, all of the old folk remedies as well, learned from her mother. With these proud bloodlines running through our veins, it's no wonder we were wanderers, healers, and seekers of truth and light. "It's in the blood!" she used to say.

By the time I was eight years old, I had come to understand that other children didn't play the same games that I did. Mostly, they didn't know what I was talking about and just looked at me blankly. Their mother's never taught them about seeing a person's aura or calling the faery folk to the garden.

On very rare occasions, I would wish to be like everyone else, but deep down inside, I knew that a life without faeries and astral travel and all the other wonderful things that we knew about wouldn't be worth living. So I held my tongue and learned to "be silent."

On this particular day, I can remember being somewhat petulant. I was bored, and I couldn't think of anything to do. I was being a brat; whining as we went along. As we approached the door of the old house, it was opened by an old lady with bright pink cheeks and a sweet smile on her face.

Looking back, she was probably only fifty or so, but to an eight-year old that's practically dead! And of course, everyone looked older in the sixties.

In Australia, ladies still wore white gloves and prim suits when they went to town, along with hats or their hair in buns. There was no individuality or colour to the world. You complied or you were ostracised.

The lady greeted my mother warmly and ushered her inside and down the hallway with its imposing photographs in heavy frames and into the sitting room. It was a friendly room, big soft seats with embroidered cushions, and I can remember lots of candles, candles everywhere; some of them in big, impressive holders. I was told to sit in here whilst my mother conducted her business.

I sat on the lounge with my feet dangling and watched as my mother was taken through to the sunroom with the large wooden table. I can remember there were flowers everywhere and all sorts of herbs and plants sitting on the shelves and hanging from the wooden rafters. Due to the open plan of the rooms I could see her clearly from my vantage point on the lounge. I liked this place; it had a good 'feel' to it. So I sat quietly and watched as my mother handed over her list of requirements.

As the nice woman left to gather the herbs on the list, two others entered the room, and after greeting my mother warmly, they sat down with her at the table, and all three started talking intently. I wasn't really listening, being engrossed by the beautiful plants and flowers that seemed to fill every space within the sunroom. "How wonderful to live here," I thought to myself.

When the older woman returned, she was carrying a brown paper bag and handed it over to my mother, who thanked her and paid the *money; then to my surprise, I was ushered into the room and told to sit at the table next to my mother.*

Mum squeezed my hand and told me I was in for a treat. I hoped it was fairy cakes and lemonade, but it would turn out to be something far more earth-shattering and life-altering. This was the moment that I was to see magick, real magick, come to life. Certainly, I was no stranger to the magickal world. Even at age eight, I knew how to cast a circle of protection. I understood that life had so much more to offer than we could see, touch or feel. My entire family had some psychic ability, and I myself possessed a kinetic ability that came and went at the oddest times and would be something that even to this day, I would have no control over; but this was different. This was real, purposeful, intentional magick, powerful, and under control. You could positively feel it in the air!

On the table stood a large wrought iron candlestick holder with one tall candle standing proudly in the centre. Candle wax in diverse colours dripped around the holder, cascading like a wax fountain down to its base. As I looked around the table, I could see that each of the women, including my mother, was staring intently at the candle. Slowly an almost inaudible chant began; rhythmic and somehow soothing to the ears. As the chant grew louder, I saw two of the women rocking back and forth whilst the third began making strange movements with her hands. Suddenly, the candle in the middle of the table came to life, bursting into flame as if on queue.

I know my mouth fell open. I could feel my mother glance down at me, but I was far too interested in what was happening to take any notice. The women smiled and looked at me; the oldest giving me a knowing wink and then they proceeded with the meeting as if nothing momentous had just happened!

My mother and I stayed for another half hour or so before we left to continue our day. I can remember pestering her to tell me what had just happened, but all she would say was that life held more questions than it did answers, and I should never be surprised by what might be possible.

From that moment onwards, I was hooked. I would spend the next 40 odd years seeking, learning, and finding my own way through a veritable sea of differing paths. Some were brilliant and enlightening, others were pure wind and bluster, but from each, I would glean whatever I could before moving on.

I have attained third degree (twice), become a student of the Kabbalah, and of high magick, and finally, now, at age 53, I have come to understand something of the crooked path. You really DO have to do it your way. It is a path that can be shown but not lived by anyone but you. So many people will try to tell you that their way is the only way to do a certain thing, but the truth is, there is always another way. Take the parts that feel right to you and make them your own, and most important of all - Make sure you find the joy and the wonder in whatever you do because this is what causes the magick to occur.

Don't let anyone or any group suck the joy out of learning the Craft, for joyous it truly is. I found my joy in learning the magickal arts and occult laws, in becoming an artist, a scribe, and an herbalist. These things please me, like my love of the ocean, trees, and animals, but most of all, I love the mysteries and wonders that life holds, and because of that, I will always be a seeker of truth and light.

The learning never ends.

* * *

About the Author

Ilana Sturm is an artist, author and witch born in Australia to a family filled with magick, lore and tradition. Over the last 30 years plus she has studied and practiced many different magickal disciplines and traidtions that have all contributed to her own personal crooked path.

Her journey has led her from the pyramids of Egypt to Stonehenge, from Glastonbury Tor to Uluru an beyond. She now spends her time at her home by the sea where she paints, grows herbs and continues her writing, hoping to pass on to the next generation some of the wisdoms she learned on the way.

Books by Ilana Sturm

    A Witch Among the Herbs (Pendraig Publishing Inc)
    The 13th Moon (Pendraig Publishing Inc)
    Idris and the Scroll of Destiny (Pendraig Publishing Inc)
    Contributor: Call of the God (TDM Publishing)

Sacred Boundaries in Pagan Practice

Pegi Eyers

The explosion of eclecticism in modern Paganism has been amazing to see! There has never been a time in human history when the magical practices of societies worldwide (including our own) have been so easy to discover and fall in love with. In recent decades, our mutual learning and creativity in spiritual seeking have led to brand-new Pagan and Polytheist genres that never existed before. And the recovery of ancient wisdom in new and vibrant traditions has dealt a powerful blow to the materialism and over-rationality of Empire. For centuries now, the imperialist system we have been forced to endure has tried to separate us from the sacred, the ineffable, and the earth emergent. But there is no stopping the perennialism of spiritual expression, and we need to celebrate all the inspired and vibrant syncretizations around us in the Pagan community today.

Yet, for all the beauty, excitement, and sense of "coming home," it has been easy to miss the complex political realities connected to the cultural practices we adore. And unless we deliberately seek out the kind of secular information that allows us to form a more nuanced snapshot of a particular society, we can be unfamiliar with important issues. In my own trajectory as a Celtic Animist, I noticed for years that the First Nations around me were recovering from the dark ages of genocide, oppression, segregation, assimilation, and residential schools. But it was only in recent times that I became fully aware of the damage cultural appropriation has also done.[1] At last! Hearing the First Nations side of the story is what turned my world around. My Animist practices were not culturally specific, but I witnessed many of my friends and colleagues in the Pagan and New Age community become blind-sided by accusations of "cultural appropriation." And being reprimanded for practices you have held dear for many years is no joke, that's for sure!

Whether you are still wondering about the difference between cultural exchange and cultural appropriation, or have been "called out" in person or online, or have read about cultural appropriation in articles and blogs, there is one simple rule to follow. **Ask yourself if the cultures are on a level footing. Is one culture is freely sharing with another, or is there an oppressor/oppressed relationship, and is the oppressor taking from the**

oppressed? The answer to this question - and the implications related to that historical and contemporary dynamic - is what will bring the controversy into focus.

The first thing we should realize is that everyone who is a descendent of the original Euro-Settler Society in the Americas (Pagans included) still belongs to the dominant group. As white folks, we have certain entitlements and hold white privilege that allows us to take elements of other cultures and identities as a normalized and unchallenged practice. Turtle Island First Nations have pretty much been invisible to us! Without proper boundaries, we have lifted elements of cultural and spiritual property from many indigenous groups in the Americas, such as rituals for creating sacred space, four directions petitioning, smudging, talking stick circles, drumming, "feather-work," vision quests, sweat lodge recreations, sacred fire gatherings, initiation rites, and the aesthetic delights of Indigenous material culture such as headdresses, wardrobe, jewelry, and décor.

These things are sacred items, ceremonies, and practices belonging to First Nations, who are still experiencing oppression every day. Taken without permission, First Nations have made it abundantly clear that this kind of appropriation interferes with the very real process of cultural recovery, healing from genocide, sovereignty-seeking, and reclaiming of tribal lands that are still going on in Indian Country. Also, from a Pagan perspective, the tokenizing, objectifying, and voyeuristic presence of First Nations (the "other") in our spaces is just as disempowering as exclusion. These practices should be reprehensible to the values that we hold.

In today's hopeful climate of First Nations resurgence, it is important to understand that cultural appropriation is the final link in the chain of erasure. Empire has enacted a colonial agenda that (1) seeks to eradicate Indigenous people, (2) takes the land and resources, and (3) erases the cultural identity of the Indigenous people themselves. When we consider the phenomena of cultural appropriation on a deep level, we see that these activities are not harmless or "spiritual" – they are the acts of the deepest racism. Did you know that the cultural markers we are drawn to, like drums, pipes, and sweat lodges, are the very same things that were outlawed by the colonial powers? What Pagans freely use in their everyday lives were things First Nations could be killed for using not that long ago. There is something extremely macabre about that.

Even having "permission" from a First Nations Elder or acting on a dream or past-life vision can carry huge ethical considerations. Spirituality with a moral code means restraint and discernment, and the integrity of focus. For example, if you have heard the ancestors of the Kogi1 "calling you" and consider yourself one of the Kogi "people," you really have to wonder if the same deities also informed the Kogi that you are part of their culture! Or, if you are convinced that your past life as Lakota, Cherokee, or Huichol gives you special insights or the entitlement to claim ancestors from those traditions, do you really need to "go public?" Perhaps it is a private matter best understood over time as you continue to explore the continuum of your personal mythology.

So, instead of participating in cultural appropriation and the systemic racism, it suggests, perhaps shifting to the authentic earth-connected wisdom traditions of one's own ancestors is a great solution! Sourcing models for earth-connected communities has been a challenge for modern Pagans, but instead of looking to the cultural and spiritual property of Indigenous people, we may find old/new templates for magical and mystic practices right in the original pre-colonial culture(s) of Old Europe. How beautiful and honoring of ourselves and ourAncestors, to re-create our specific traditional roots to the best of our ability!

Of course, we will always owe a huge debt to the flourishing of cultural pluralism, new spiritualities, and healthy life-sustaining practices in our time. These are now features of society we take for granted, but unfortunately, within the gigantic transformational Pagan and New Age marketplace, the genre of "Native Spirituality" has been normalized. Calling out cultural appropriation requires us to question these activities, even though they are widespread and found in many spaces such as workshops, Pagan bookstores, and metaphysical shops. Calling out cultural appropriation requires us to question these activities, even though they are widespread and found in many spaces such as workshops, Pagan bookstores, and metaphysical shops. When white academics and New Age or Pagan practitioners (those with advantage and power) write, speak or teach about the cultural and spiritual traditions of Indigenous societies, they are, in fact **dominating** the original *Indigenous Knowledge* (IK). Their versions then become the valid narratives, fabrications that are sold back to the white majority. This kind of cultural appropriation suggests disempowerment and a loss of basic human dignity and undermines Indigenous efforts to preserve their own traditions. Having control over one's autonomy and how one is perceived in the public domain is a fundamental right for every human being!

As Pagans and Polytheists, our exciting journey of revitalization continues, but we can certainly learn from our mistakes and do so much better. As we travel along our spiritual paths and refine our values as contemporary Pagan people, mending our fractured relationship with First Nations - the original holders of earth wisdom - through social justice solidarity can easily become our goal. And in the sacred reclaiming of magic, spirit, and self-identity, no one can make a decision for anyone else. But considering an ethical code and/or following a moral compass is always a good idea!

With love from Pegi Eyers.

Notes

[1] In terms of offering solutions to my Pagan and New Age cohort, I began to thoroughly investigate the ins and outs of cultural appropriation in 2012, which eventually led to a full-length book.

[2] The "People of the Earth," otherwise known as the Kogi (Cogui, Kagaba) are an Indigenous group that live in the mountains of the Sierra Nevada de Santa Marta in northern Columbia. Their culture and stewardship of the land has existed since pre-Columbian times.

About the Author

Pegi Eyers is the author of the award-winning book *Ancient Spirit Rising: Reclaiming Your Roots & Restoring Earth Community*, a survey on the interface between Turtle Island First Nations and the Settler Society, social justice, sacred land, nature spirituality, earth-emergent healing, and the principles of sustainable living. Pegi self-identifies as a Celtic Animist and is an advocate for the recovery of authentic ancestral wisdom and traditions for all people. She lives in the countryside on the outskirts of Nogojiwanong in Michi Saagiig Nishnaabeg territory (Peterborough, Ontario, Canada), on a hilltop with views reaching for miles in all directions. www.stonecirclepress.com

Ancient Spirit Rising is the recipient of a 2017 Next Generation Indie Book Award in the Current Events/Social Change category! With 420 pages, full colour, extensive notes, live links and exhaustive references, the PDF Download of Ancient Spirit Rising is "A Compendium for Change!"

Join our FB Group for sharing on social justice, nature spirituality and the Ancestral Arts. www.facebook.com/groups/18635920508609

Of Wine and Sabbats

Hillary Klein

We in the Pagan community have been blessed with some of the most incredible rites, some ancient and some a little more nouveau in style, but no matter how you slice it, they all end up with a feast at some point, filled with delicious food and wine…NEVER forget the wine!

We also have some amazing cooks who attend our rituals bearing food literally fit for the Gods, but what about the wine? How does one pick wines befitting the Gods that pair with the food, are easy to find, and without busting one's budget? How about if you could bring great altar-worthy wines for under $20?

Well, here is where I come in. I'm not only a part of this incredible community, but I am also a Sommelier and a Wine and Spirits Educator.

First, let's look at some of the upcoming Sabbats/rituals for this year and break down some of the foods that would typically be served, along with their significance. In this volume of the journal, we are looking at Summer Solstice through Samhain. With that in mind, let's look at what those would be.

We will be looking at Litha/Summer Solstice, Lughnasadh/Lammas, Mabon/Autumnal Equinox, and Samhain/Halloween (my personal favorite).

Summer Solstice/Litha

When it comes to ritual foods, we are, in reality, using the bounties associated with each season. So, when we start with a Sabbat like Litha or Summer Solstice, we are talking about summer foods. Foods bright in the colors of the sun; juicy yellow and orange summer fruits and vegetables, red heirloom tomatoes added to a crisp green salad, summer squashes, cucumbers, and corn. The idea being, foods that tend to cool you down after a long day in the hot sun. Consider something like cold cucumber soup with a side of pumpernickel bread. It's also a great opportunity to grill some yummy meats over the bbq fire or enjoy some light white fish.

Naturally, we have traditional drinks that have historically been imbibed, such as meads and ales. But what about the wine? Some of the best wines, in my opinion, would be something traditionally chilled… aromatic Albarino, and sweet Moscato, higher acid Pinot Grigio/Gris (same grape just, the former is traditionally grown in Italy and the latter in France), a light style Chardonnay such as a Chablis, unoaked or neutral oaked Chardonnay and you could even throw a lovely rosé into the action. For the meats, I'd say going with lighter thin-skinned grapes like Pinot Noir, Gamay (also known as Beaujolais), or a Valdiguié (known as the "Napa Gamay") maybe even a Grenache. But, if you want something a bit heavier, you could always throw in Merlot and Zinfandel (the red one, not the "white" one), which we will discuss further down in the article.

Some recommendations would be:

Albarino:

Martin Codax Albarino - Attractive floral aromatics and brisk acidity on the palate with added flavors of pear, passion fruit, ripe apple, peach, and lemon zest framed by bright minerality and hints of spice. Average price $15

Tangent - Bursting with aromas of lemon, citrus, peach, and roses. It's crisp, vibrant, and mouthwatering with hints of minerality and fresh brininess. Average price $17

Paco & Lola Albarino – Fine notes of white fruit (green apples, pear) and lemony aromas, hints of herbs (basil), and flower blossom form the base notes. The palate is seductive with exotic pineapple and mango intermingled with refreshing citrus flavors amplified by minerally accents. Average price $19

Moscato:

Bartinura - Slightly effervescent or "frizzante," with notes of wildflowers, ripe melons, and honey followed by flavors of pear, nectarines, and apricot. Average price $13

Risata Moscato D'asti – This is seductively sweet with vibrant flavors and aromas of juicy stone fruit, tangerines, tart citrus, and floral honey flavors. Its fresh, fragrant, and frizzante concentrated flavor are not overly rich or heavy. Average price $15

Castoro Cellars Moscato – Aromas of juicy peaches, ripe apricots, white flowers; to that, a splash of Orange Muscat wine is blended in and shows tangerine peel and honeycomb notes. Average price $12

Pinot Grigio/Gris:

3 Pears-This wine is bright, balanced, and delicious. Its inviting aroma of grapefruit, pear, Meyer lemon, white flowers, and baked apple has flavors of fresh tart green apple, unripe pear, and nectarine and is rounded out by a grassy, honeyed-sweet finish. Average price $8

Cavit Pinot Grigio delle Venezie IGT – It has a crisp, light character with delicate aromas of spring blossom and white stone fruit. On the palate, crisp acidity accompanies Anjou pear and yellow apple. ~ Kerin O'keefe Average price $8

J Dusi- A clean, crisp wine with bright lychee and tart tropical fruits are balanced by its acidity, tailed by a lingering apricot finish. It showcases the bright fruit and natural acidity. Average price $13.

Chardonnay:

Four Vines 2019 Naked Chardonnay (Central Coast) – This Chardonnay has all the tropical hallmarks of the style, starting with jasmine and guava flesh on the nose. The palate generously shows pineapple, lychee, guava, and stone fruit that linger into the grippy finish. ~ MATT KETTMANN Average price $11

Bogle– Light in style with aromatic notes of yellow apple and pear, nutmeg, vanilla, pineapple, and guava, while honeycomb and vanilla heighten the first impression. The mouth is filled with Asian pears, apples, lemon, kiwi, and the finishes like the wafting aromas of grandma's warm apple pie. Average price $8

Mer Soleil Silver Unoaked Chardonnay - Opening with clean, fresh scents of kiwi, citrus zest, and nectarine that are followed up with mineral characteristics and flavors of lemon squares, a faint smokiness finishing with fresh traces of lemon and lime. Average price $16

Rosé:

La Vielle Ferme – This little rosé punches waaaay above its price point. Pale pink in color offers a fresh, delicate aroma of red fruits (currant, cherry) and citrus (lemon). On the palate, it shows beautiful notes of fresh fruit. A true find. Average price $6

Gerard Bertrand Cote de Rosés –Fresh with aromas of summer fruits, cassis, and redcurrant.

Floral notes of rose along with hints of grapefruit complete the picture. On the palate, it is fresh, offering notes of candy. Average price $13

Opolo Rosé – This is a delightfully drinkable wine that I describe as tropical fruit wrapped in a strawberry with a kiss of sweetness. Average price $18

Pinot Noir:

Hahn - Aromas of red and dark cherry, dried raspberry, and rhubarb pie with subtle touches of spice and toasty oak. On the palate notes of earthiness with a lingering finish. Average price $11

Erath- Bouquets of marionberry jam, Bing cherry, Pluot, and a hint of wintergreen meld with savory meatiness. The palate is packed full of juicy fresh raspberry, huckleberry, and blackberry, finishing with a cherry candy followed up with hints of warm spice. Average price $17

Fossil Point Pinot Noir - Dark and bold, with juicy black cherry and ripe plum aromas. This Pinot is spice-driven, with clove, orange rind, and pomegranate notes on the palate. Average price $15

Gamay:

Georges Duboeuf Beaujolais Villages Nouveau- Intensely aromatic, it has notes of red and black fruit with a subtle note of candy. It is pure and fresh on the palate with a fruity finish. Average price $15

J. Lohr Valdiguié - Bright and youthful with profuse brambly fruit aromas accented by black pepper notes. On the palate, a zesty attack of pomegranate and blueberry; leaves crisp, fresh fruit and a touch of spice on the finish. Average price $10

Louis Jadot Beaujolais - This plump, juicy wine has the fresh aroma and flavors of strawberries and black cherries offset by lively, peppery notes. Average price $10

Grenache / Garnacha:

Joel Gott Alakai Grenache – Opening with aromas of cherry cola and red berries and layered over subtle floral notes, the palate has luscious strawberry and bright cherry flavors framed by earthy undertones and notes of pepper. Average price $16

La Sonriente Garnacha - Begins with a deep aroma of red cherry, black cherry, and cranberry along with a bit of leather, wintergreen, and a touch of baking spice. It starts with ripe red fruit in the mouth, with a bit of earthiness leading into hints of tobacco and cola. ~ Jon Thorsen. Average price $10

Broken Earth Grenache - Ripe aromas of caramel-soaked cherry, vanilla candy, and toasty oak show on the nose. Those vanilla and caramel elements pop on the palate leading into rounded red-fruit flavors with hints of wild thyme and pepper on the finish. ~ Matt Kettmann. Average price $16

Lughnasadh/Lammas

As the Wheel of the Year turns, we come upon Lughnasadh (also known as Lammas - meaning Loaf Mass) to honor Lugh, the warrior Sun King; with a feast of food consisting of breads and grains (corn in particular), that is the first harvest of Autumn as it comes upon us. With the stunning colors of turning leaves and the joyous childhood feelings brought on by reminiscing of playing in the sprinkler or jumping into the leaf mounds piled up high after raking the yard. A time to celebrate the love of those wishing to be handfasted yet offset by a plea for a plentiful harvest just before we move into the colder and more desolate months of fall and winter and the need for food to hold us through them.

This time of year is also an especially important time in the vineyard. This is the time of year when veraison occurs, the time when the grapes begin to mature, and things like organic acids, sugar, polyphenols (naturally occurring micronutrients), aromas, and flavors begin to develop. This is especially noticeable in red grape varietals. They begin to ripen and start to turn from green to red, signaling to the viticulturists and vintners that picking is only a month or so away.

When pairing wines for Lughnasadh (or in general), we look to the foods being served to make sure to use complementary or contrasting flavors to enhance them. Breads, cakes and cookies, fresh summer fruits like pears, melons, berries, stone fruits; and green leafy vegetables, yellow corn, red tomatoes served with meats like fish, lamb, and chicken – though, very little meat is meant to be consumed during this celebration.

Fun Fact: When dealing with sweeter foods like cakes, cookies, and fruit pies, typically, we want to match them with wines that should be equally sweet or sweeter than the food; otherwise, the wines can taste bitter and acidic.

Since the days are longer and tend to be warmer, I would recommend starting off the balmy evening with chilled, lighter style and semi-sweet, aromatic wines like Gewurztraminer, Torrontés and Rieslings or even anything from a brand like Stella Rosa (what I call the "kool aid" of wines) with their fruit-infused, effervescent style. These wines can not only be cooling and refreshing but also pair beautifully with some of the sweeter and savory style treats and the vegetable (especially if it's spicy) based fare being served. As the evening progresses into night and the feasting begins, wines that are a bit weightier and have more complexity can be served, such as a nice creamy Chardonnay or a pretty Merlot. There is even the option to throwback to the wines from Litha, as they also would be ideally suited for the weather and festival theme.

So, to that end, some of the more generalized recommendations would be:

Gewurztraminer:

Trader Joe's Petit Reserve Gewurztraminer - Having aromas of stone fruits, lychee, citrus, and tropical fruits with notes of honeysuckle, this wine is a perfect complement to some of the sweeter fare served at this festival. Average price $8

Fetzer Gewurztraminer - This wine has some complex aromas of tangerine, mango, and orange spice, leading up to rich flavors of baked pears, caramelized apples, and pineapple, spiced with hints of cinnamon and clove. Average price $8

Husch Gewurtztraminer Anderson Valley - Intense floral aromas of rose petal, gardenia, and honeysuckle couple with the subtle, perfumed spice notes of ginger and green tea. In the mouth, the wine confirms its floral and spice character and shows zesty citrus and concentrated lychee-nut. Average price $12

Rieslings:

Firestone - Showing aromas of citrus blossom, honeysuckle, and green tea, leading into a palate showing citrus notes with lemon tart characteristics and topped off by a bright, lively acidity. Average price $9

Kendall Jackson - Crisp with layers of apricot, peach, hints of Anjou pear, and orange blossom blend with bursts of aromatic jasmine and a wonderful finish. Average price $11

For something a bit on the drier side and with more versatility for a cross-section of foods…

Dr. Loosen Dr. L Riesling - From the Mosel region of Germany, it is one of the most recognized names in Riesling. It's low alcohol and is refreshing and fruity with crisp aromas of citrus fruit, ripe pear, and a note of spice with a fine mineral edge. It is brightly fruit-driven and juicy. Average price $13

Kung Fu Girl - Made in a drier style and showing white peach, mandarin orange, and apricot with a core of minerality, it shimmers with energy and freshness. Average price $13

Torrontés:

Maipe Torrontes - Bouquets of fresh white peaches, pears, green apple, green melon, and hints of jasmine and rose petals lead into a beautiful palate of fruit flavors and a pleasant freshness with citrus notes. Average price $13

Alamos Torrontes - With lively notes of citrus and peach fruit interwoven with layers of delicate jasmine blossom and fresh herbs. It sits lightly and fresh on the palate. Average price $10

Bodega Colome Torrontes - Enrobing floral notes of roses with a citrus aroma of grapefruit and a hint of spice, the mouth is reminiscent of Muscat with notes of jasmine and orange blossoms. Average price $15

Chardonnay:

Raeburn - Presenting an array of complex fruit tones ranging from pear and Gravenstein apple to nectarine, the fruit is beautifully complemented with toasted oak, vanilla, and hints of crème brûlée. Average price $18

Chateau St. Jean Creamy - Aromas of ripe tropical fruit are enhanced by flavors of crème brûlée, spiced apple, and lemon meringue on the buttery palate. Average price $8

Daou - Notes of honeysuckle and vanilla complement fragrances of tropical fruit and warm toast, Bosc pear, pineapple, and guava with hints of hibiscus flower, white peach, and allspice. The palate is lush with mouth-filling flavors of sweet honeydew melon, mango, pineapple, and creamy vanilla crème brûlée. Complementary flavors of citrus and nectarine are accented by suggestions of hazelnut and toasted almonds throughout. Average price $17

Merlot:

Rodney Strong - Lush with predominant notes of blackberries, black cherry, and plum, with a hint of dried herbs. Silky and voluptuous with dark fruit and a touch of dried cocoa and vanilla. Average price $16

Ancient Peaks – The bouquets of dusty boysenberry, black cherry, vanilla, slate, and toasted oak lead to mouth-filling flavors of plump blueberry, blackberry, raspberry, cinnamon, dark chocolate, and cola. Average price $18

St Francis – Deep garnet in color with a fruit-forward profile of cherry, blackberries, plum, and mocha on the nose and lush flavors of cherries, baking spices, mocha, blue, and blackberries. Average price $17

Mabon/Autumn Equinox

Mabon, also known as the Autumnal Equinox, is when the symbols of male fertility and masculine energy make itself known as it embraces the fields and grips the season. This is the time of year when we tend to start drinking wines that are more masculine in style. So, what does that mean? What makes a wine masculine versus feminine?

Think of masculine wines as being bigger and bolder, more expressive, more muscular and "in your face," and less restrained in style, where feminine wines are more light, delicate, nuanced, and soft with a refined elegance.

A good comparison would be a big, heavy, bold and brooding, higher alcohol, tannic Napa Cabernet Sauvignon versus a bright, aromatic, delicately floral, lower alcohol, spritzy sweet Moscato d'Asti.

Mabon is the time when we begin to wind down and become introspective; the long days start to get darker sooner as the sun's summer light makes its way to the Southern Hemisphere. As our memories of laying by the pool and the feeling of toes in the sand by the seaside subside; we are hitting the height of the grape harvest. Many of the wines made of this vintage will grace the dinner table by this same time next year.

Speaking of the dinner table, this is the time to bring forth the root vegetables, nuts, wheat-based products, anything made with pome fruits, corn, sweet potatoes, squash (especially pumpkin), pomegranates, beans…and GRAPES!!

Now is the time to free your frenzied self, seize on masculine energy, and ecstatically. Honor the gods of the vine!

Which wines will pair best with all this masculine infused ecstasy? As mentioned, Napa (and Paso) Cabs are a great go-to, but we could also add Tempranillo, Syrah, and medium to full-bodied Pinots to the list; as for whites, we can go with Sauvignon Blanc and bring on those big, oaky, buttery Chards. Some great wines to consider pairing are:

Sauvignon Blanc:

Sea Glass - with aromas of lemon, lime, grapefruit, and crisp palate of gooseberry, tangerine, and a touch of minerality. Average price $8

Pommelo – It's lively, refreshing, and crisp with aromas of white blossoms and flavors of peach, melon & citrus. Average price $9

Nobilo – Showing flavors of pineapple, elderflower, cantaloupe, and citrus. It's fresh, bright, balanced, and always crisp. Straight out of Marlborough, New Zealand. Average price $10

Chardonnay:

Butter - Rich, bold and luscious, brimming with stone fruit and baked-lemon notes complimented by a lush creaminess and vanilla finish. Average price $15

R. Mondavi Buttery - Decadent aromas of ripe pineapples and crème brûlée and lush flavors of apple, graham crackers, and white peach paired with rich, creamy flavors of butter, brown spice, toasted oak, and vanilla. Average price $9

Acacia - Offering bright aromas of ripe stone fruit, lemon peel, mandarin spice, and tones of warm honeycomb, then packed with layers of baked apple and pear, green apple, white peach with hazelnut and crème caramel flavors that expand across the palate. A classic CA chardonnay. Average price $15

Cabernet Sauvignon:

St. Hubert's The Stag - Blueberry, brown sugar, sweet-fruit, plum, and blackberry aromas persist with hints of dark chocolate, elderberry, and nutmeg characters. Packed with black, red, and blue fruit, complemented by notes of stewed capsicum, pepper, and spice with subtly layered fruit. The luxuriant palate is lush with black currant and vanilla with plenty of intense blueberry/ mocha/cocoa notes. Full, ripe, balanced with robust dark fruit/dark chocolate flavors and underlying savory oak. Average price $17

Borne of Fire - A downright delicious red that has loads of sweet red and blue fruits, hints of spring flowers, no hard edges, and a great texture. ~ *Jeb Dunnuck* Average price $19

Bread and Butter - Ripe and robust with layers of mocha, fresh berries, blackcurrant, and subtle black pepper, toasted oak, and rich vanilla. Round and luscious with a hint of spice. Average price $14

Syrah:

Qupe - Deep purple, with aromas of blackberry, black raspberries, and hints of cola and leather. The flavors are savory with a spicy, smoky character, refreshing, juicy, and a touch of French oak. Average price $16

Boom Boom – Aromas of fresh boysenberry, white pepper, fresh-picked herbs, and wet earth. Spicy and bold flavors of rich black cherry, blackberry, and tobacco are followed by hints of lavender. Average price $16

Castoro Reserve Whale Rock – Starting with aromas of cured meats, black currants, and licorice with a palate of wood smoke, black fruit, plum, and bacon fat. Average price $19

Tempranillo (Rioja):

Marques De Riscal - Expressive aromas on the nose hosting notes of licorice, cinnamon, and black pepper, with just a subtle hint of the long cask-aging thanks to its incredible complexity and ripe, concentrated fruit. Average price $19

Campo Viejo Rioja – A nose rich in aromas and struck by ripe red fruit, wood nuances, and gentle, sweet notes of vanilla with other sweet spices. The palate is perfumed, soft, and fresh, with a long finish leaving memories of red fruit, vanilla, and cocoa. Average price $9

Marques De Caceres Creanza – A nice, deep bouquet of fine toasted wood and spices, combined with red candied fruit on a licorice base. Full-bodied on the palate with a background of ripe fruit. Average price $15

Pinot Noir:

Meiomi - The wine opens to reveal fruit aromas of bright strawberry and jammy fruit, mocha, and vanilla, along with toasty oak notes. Expressive boysenberry, blackberry, dark cherry, juicy strawberry, and toasty mocha flavors lend complexity and depth to the palate. Average price $19.99

Elouan - Dark ruby red in color, this wine opens with aromas of dark cherry, persimmon, dark chocolate, and sweet pipe tobacco. The palate is rich, robust, and intense with flavors of Bing cherry, cocoa, candied cranberry, and boysenberry. Average price $18

Beringer Founder's Estate - This medium- to full-bodied wine shows classic black and red-cherry aromas, a broad palate of dark fruits, and light oak spices. *~Jim Gordon*. Average price $10

Samhain

Now comes one of the most important Sabbats, when the veil between the worlds is thinnest. The time when little ghosts and goblins go trick-or-treating and squeals of delight fill the air, yet also when the Pagan world becomes even more introspective and sets aside time to honor all the ancestors and those that have passed on through the year. Samhain (All Hallows Eve, Halloween) rites are a way to set intentions, divine the future, commune carving jack-o-lanterns, and celebrating with all the foods of the final harvest: grains, pumpkins, cranberries, apples, pomegranates, root vegetables, herbs, and hearty meat dishes.

In addition, this is the time to finish picking the last of the grapes off the vine and those set aside as "late harvest" to develop higher brix (sugar) content for the sweet, dessert wines to come.

As the temperatures, drop it's also a good time to drink heavier, more complex, and higher alcohol wines that can have savory, spicy, meaty notes that stand up to heartier meals. Wines like Zinfandel, Petite Sirah, full-bodied Pinots, bold Bordeaux varietals (Cabernet Sauvignon, Merlot, Malbec, Petit Verdot, Carménère and Cab Franc) and Rhone Style wines (Grenache, Syrah, Mourvèdre to name a few) and other bold red blends. As for whites, we call back to big, oaky Chardonnays, Viogniers, and Grüner Veltliners, and lastly, dessert Ports, Sherries, and Late Harvest wines that come in both red and white varietals.

Chardonnay:

Wente Riva Ranch - opens with bold oak aromatics, complemented by rich tropical fruit such as pineapple to white nectarine and sweet baking spices on the palate. Average price $16

Mirassou Sun - has a fruit-forward bouquet showing intense layers of nectarine, peach, and tropical fruit—with added flavors of peaches, pineapple, melon, pears, floral, and vanilla with notes of oak and citrus. Average price $8

J Lohr Riverstone Chardonnay - exhibits enticing aromas of white peach, apricot, ripe orange, and cocoa, complemented by a palate full of citrus cream and nectarine, giving way to flavors of vanilla, crème brûlée, and a touch of oak. Average price $12

Grüner Veltliner:

Floriana Gruner Veltliner - Fresh and lively with appetizing aromas of lemon and apple and just a touch of white pepper, leading into a palate filled with lime, pineapple, and green apple. It ends with delightful hints of green peppers and freshly mowed grass. Average price $6

Zocker - A pronounced minerality and bright aromas of lemon and lime on the nose, a strong white pepper note, and flavors of ripe melon and fruit cocktail. Average price $17

Joel Gott - Aromas of Bartlett pear, white pepper, and notes of fresh honey transition to a palate of citrus notes followed by ripe fruit flavors on the mid-palate with a hint of spice and a refreshing finish with notes of butterscotch. Average price $18

Viognier:

Vina Robles - Bouquets of ripe apple and floral notes meld with bright and delicious peach, mandarin orange zest, and hints of honeysuckle and ginger. The flavors burst with lively peach, citrus flowers, and ripe apples. Average price $16

Cline Cellars - A rich, perfumed varietal; it shows pineapple, peach, and apricot flavors, with accents of floral and citrus notes. Average price $12

Domaine Astruc 'dA' - Rich and elegant with dry fruits, peach, and white flower aromas and a hint of vanilla/ honey notes. Fresh and mellow with a long persistence finishing on toasted notes. Average price $13

Zinfandel:

Tobin James Ballistic - Full-bodied and delicious, the fruit aroma leads one into a palate bursting with notes of cherries, spices, oak, smoke, berries, pepper, vanilla, currants, & tobacco. Average price $16

7 Deadly Zins - Full-bodied and seductive with heaps of jammy berry fruit followed by aromas of leather, oak and spice notes. The wine is round and layered on the palate, showing flavors of dark fruits, currants, and toffee through a lingering spice-touched finish. $14

Four Vines – Ripe, wild berry flavors with a hefty dusting of spice and zesty pepper, offering wild raspberry and ripe black cherry flavors with slightly stewed dark bramble fruits, ripe, smoky blackberry, and spiced, soft fruit followed by a warming finish. Average price $10

Cabernet / Merlot/ Malbec:

Ferrari-Carano Merlot - Velvety with a complex nose of plum, cherry, cedar, black peppercorn, and pomegranate followed by an enticing palate with flavors of black huckleberries, dried currants, leather, and clove. Average price $19

Right Hand Man Cabernet Sauvignon - Powerful aromas of cherry, cassis, and dark chocolate are lifted by a peppery element that gains strength with air. Sweet and seamless on the palate, offering pliant dark fruit and chewing tobacco flavors and a sweet vanilla quality. Average price $19

Alamos Wine Malbec - Deeply concentrated plum, dark cherry, and blackberry flavors with well integrated hints of brown spice and vanilla. Average price $10

Petite Sirah/Syrah:

Victor Hugo Petite Sirah - Delightful aroma profile best described as "spice rack" meets ripe plums. Fresh ground black pepper, bay leaf, and clove predominate with rich plum notes in the background and toasty oak followed by an extended, rich finish. Average price $18

Michael David Winery Petite Petit - Showcasing aromas of dark fruit, raspberry, and fig, this wine is layered with rich flavors of black cherry, cola, and light oak on the palate. Average price $18

Zaca Mesa Syrah - Concentrated black fruits are outlined by freshly churned soil, wild herbs, and smoked meat. The dense middle palate carries lingering flavors of vibrant blackberry and sweet oak spice. $18

Blends:

Chronic Cellars Purple Paradise - A roasted red-plum aroma meets with savory leather and dried beef jerky on the nose of this Zin-based bottling. On the palate, roasted strawberry, cinnamon, and pie crust flavors. ~ *Matt Kettmann* Average price $14

Phantom (by Bogle) - Aromas of baked cherry cobbler and ripe cranberries are front and center. Framed with nutmeg and allspice, all wrapped up with peppercorn, anise, and juniper berries. Average price $19

Apothic - Generous notes of blueberry, plum, and subtle spice finish with long-lasting notes of soft vanilla and mocha create an intriguing intensity. Average price $10

Hahn GSM - Enticing aromas of blueberry and strawberry jam come to the fore, followed by cedar and a hint of exotic spice. The palate delivers layers of bright cherry, strawberry, white pepper, and cinnamon. Average price $14

Pinot Noir:

BÖEN - Aromas of dark plum and white pepper and framed by dry Italian herbs with notes of cinnamon and clove spices. Abundant blackberry bramble and touches of maraschino cherry fill the mid-palate. Average price $19

Angeline Vineyards - Fruit forward with vivid notes of cranberry, raspberry and dark cherry, cola, and toasted oak. Average price $11

La Crema Sonoma - Aromas of red cherry, pomegranate, and sweet tobacco are followed by flavors of assorted berries, plum, and subtle toasted notes. Average price $18

Late Harvest & Dessert Style Wines:

Hogue Late Harvest Riesling - A sweet, mouthwatering white wine with notes of tangerine, honey, and honeysuckle, with a hint of minerality. Zesty aromas of orange, lemon-lime and peach are followed by flavors of tangerine, apricot, and a trace of mineral. Average price $7

Tobin James Liquid Love - Sweet and lush, showcasing a very seductive aroma of sweet black fruits; very ripe on the palate with a rich sweetness. Average price $18

Sandeman Ruby Port – Brilliant red ruby in color, with clean aromas of red fruits, plums, and strawberries, full, rich flavors with overt notes of fresh plums and red fruits. Average price $15

Fonseca Porto Wine Bin 27 - Intense, rich, fruity nose crammed with pure blackberry, cassis, cherry, and plum aromas interwoven with spice notes. The palate's juicy black fruit flavors linger into the rich, luscious finish. Average price $15

Harvey's Bristol Cream - The nose is fragrant with fruity aromatic notes of raisins and hints of caramel. On the palate, it is smooth, creamy, and highlights the fruitiness. Average price $15

*****Bodega Dios Bacos Oxford Pedro Xiemenez Sherry** - Thick and intense, full of raisins, honeyed figs, and dried prunes. Some chocolate and Spanish pan de higos and hints of coffee and sticky toffee. The palate is very smooth and velvety, almost buttery. It shows a classic mixture of prunes, figs, and cocoa again with Belgian pear syrup and a hinted lemon note but it's almost wholly overrun by sticky sweetness and a slight pinch of pepper on the finish. Average price $18

*There are several types and styles of Sherry; this one is very rich and syrupy in texture and is perfect for the season, and a perfect pairing for the decadent dried fruit and spice cakes often served going into the Yuletide. If it's not your style, don't be turned off by Sherry, there are many that have different tastes, weights, and textures. Spend some time tasting through the different types until you find one that you like.

* * *

Even with these guidelines and recommendations, I always try and encourage others to try the various wines with different foods to see which ones pair best with each dish. A simple rule of thumb is "What grows together, goes together" and will rarely fail you in a pinch.

Pairing takes practice, so to that end, some attempts will be absolute gems, and others will be total duds, but you'll never know unless you try them. Don't be afraid to experiment with wine styles, varietals, and food. When you get the right pairing…you will absolutely know!

Lastly, and more important than anything else, no matter what I or anyone else says, the BEST wine is simply the wine you like best.

Wine Pronunciation Guide:

Beaujolais - boh jhoe lay

Cabernet Sauvignon - cab er nay saw vee nyon

Carménère - kär-me-`ner

Chardonnay - shar doh nay

Chablis - shah blee

Chenin Blanc - shen in blahnk

Gewurztraminer – guh vurts tra mee ner

Grenache – greh nash / Garnacha – Gar na cha

Grüner Veltliner - grew-ner velt-LEE-ner.

Malbec – maal bek

Merlot - mer loh

Moscato d'Asti – muh skaa tow d ah sti

Mourvedre - mohr-VED-dra and more-VED (both are acceptable)

Pedro Ximenez – pei drow zi muh nez

Pinot Grigio – pee noh GREE joe

Pinot Gris - pee noh gree

Pinot Noir - pee·now nuh·waar

Riesling- REESE ling

Sauvignon Blanc - saw vee nyon blahnk

Tempranillo - tem prah NEE yoh

Torrontés - toh-ROHN-tehs

Valdiguié - val-di-gu-ie

Viognier – VEE-own-YAY

- Please remember that in general wines change with the vintages (the year the grapes are harvested) but I have tried to stay with brands that are fairly consistent from year to year.

- Credit: Jamie Wood and Tara Seefeldt authors of the Wicca Cookbook, as well as www.reversewinesnob.com, Wilfred Wong. www.dummies.com/food-drink/drinks/wine/how-to-pronounce-wine-names, www.sherrynotes.com/2013/reviews/pedro-ximenez/oxford-1970-px-dios-baco/ and the wine makers notes of some of the various wines discussed. In addition, the critics are notated, though some notes have been truncated, paraphrased or adjusted for brevity.

∼

About the Author

Hillary Klien has been apracticing witch for over 25 years. She is a Level 1 Sommelier and a Level 2 certified WSET with Distinction and has channeled her enthusiam, knowledge and performance expierience into educating people about wine and the wine scene.

Language of the Mind

Soledad Osraige

The water frightened me. When I was small, my father, whom I barely remember, would lift and carry me down to a dock that extended long out into the river. And it was deep and green and completely opaque; so at odds with the tall apartments behind us. We looked across the wide water and I remember gasping, feeling what it would be like to fall into that water from the dock, several feet above the surface and float in the current, and be lost.

"I won't let that happen," Father said. "Besides," he continued, "I grew up on the water, sailing boats like those you see across in New Jersey," he pointed, "So I've fallen in this river many times. And I've survived it. I'll teach you to swim. But I won't do it here, because now, unlike when I was your age, the water is too dirty. Damn the polluters." He cursed and said what sounded like "magar," something in another language I didn't know.

"What did you say, Father?" I asked him. But he just shook his head.

"That's not English."

He said simply, "No, it's Rom and you don't need to know that." He looked so severe that I didn't question, although I had heard my father's sisters speaking it and my mother singing in Irish and longed to know what the words meant. "You've got to speak English, girlie."

"I do speak English, Father. But I want...."

"No." He said sharply, and I stopped trying.

"Look," He said, "You've got my hair," ruffling my black curls, "and your mother's eyes, and they will get you far in this world. But if you start speaking Rom or the Gaelic, life will be hard for you." We stood looking downriver toward the city, New York City, for a while. Then my father lifted me, kissed me on the forehead, and set me back on my feet. "Now, run along home," He said, "I've got to get to work." I turned and began to walk away. At the corner, I stopped to look back

at him, but he was gone. And in my memory, that was the last time I saw him. I had walked back home, to meet my older brother Isaac coming in from his baseball practice. His good friend Finn, whom I secretly loved, was with him and they were drinking milk, and eating cookies that our Grandmother Radha had made. She was sitting in her rocking chair, smiling her lovely smile. Finn handed me a glass of milk and a sugar cookie.

Radha said to us all, "Tell me about your school today," but she looked at me, and I leaned against her lap.

Instead of answering, I asked her, "Grandma, won't you teach me your language?"

She frowned. "No, I can't, my doll, your parents won't allow it," and as my father had, she muttered some word foreign to me. "Someday, you'll learn, so be easy about it. So come, tell me about your school."

I thought about it, hesitating. I watched Isaac and Finn begin to study together. I felt like I had to make something up. Did I? thinking about my classes. "We learned in history about when different people came to the new world, and how they spoke all different languages. Some learned English, like our people, were forced to do when the English took over our country. But some stayed in small groups and made their own worlds and excluded others. "

"Do you think that was good, child?" She asked.

"Yes," I answered. "Look at how our people were forced to be slaves to the English and they took our language and customs? That wasn't right!" I said firmly.

Her smile faded. "My bright golden angel. That's not what you learned in school." I saw that Finn watched me from the corner of his eye. I leaned closer to Radha and smelled her perfume."Did you even go to school today? She whispered. "You can tell me."

"Oh, I did," I replied honestly. And I truly had. My mind wandered in class; I scratched in my notebook; dreams, spells, and just whatever came to me. I turned the page when the teacher came around, hating her watchful eyes. She knew I was making up my own lessons, but there was a look in her eye that approved, coming from deep within her. After class one day, she handed me a small book with a black cover. The Mabinogion, it said. On my way home that day, on the subway, I began reading. Now, I slipped it from where it was hidden in my notebook and showed it to my Grandmother.

"Ah, that," She patted my hand, "that's from the Welsh. They're our distant neighbors. Cousins, if you will. Many of them have hair like yours. Is there a tale in it that you like best?

'Oh...Blodeuwedd, the owl queen. And Branwen. And King Arthur's tale, of course, it's so sad. Grandma, do you know the Welsh language too?"

"No, I don't," she said.

"I wish Father would let me learn another language.' I whispered to her.

Her arm came around my shoulder and she pulled me close. In my ear, she whispered. "I can teach you the language of the trees, the stones, and the water if you like."

"Yes!" I said, hushed.

"No one would know except the two of us." She said back to me, her voice also low. "It's a language of the mind." I sat further onto her lap and our foreheads pressed together. "I taught your mother too, so she can't object to it. And we don't have to tell your father. Would you like a lesson now?"

My eyes shone. "I would indeed!'

"Put your books away and change your school clothes and meet me in the study."

I whispered again, "Can you teach Finn also?"

Radha smiled and said, "Someday, child, you'll teach him." She kissed my cheek. "Go, change."

* * *

"A Language of the Mind was written to explore the childhood of the heroine in my upcoming novel, North River Magic"

Soledad Osraige

About the Author Soledad Osraige

Soledad is an author and feral cat advocate living in New Jersey. Her first novel, **North River Magic,** is due to be published by Cynefin Road Books in the fall of 2021.

Facebook: Soledad Osraige

Instagram: Soledad.osraige

Tumblr: https://soledad-osraige.tumblr.com

An excerpt from

Journey to the Castle

By Ann Finnin

New Release from Pendraig Publishing Inc

August 2021, CE

Yes, animal masks were certainly used at one time by shamans. However, an animal mask does not a shaman make. Nor does it automatically confer upon the wearer true totem animal powers no matter how long one dances around a circle.

This is why, 10,000 years ago, the shaman put on his deer hide and antlered headdress that either he or someone in his tribe had killed and skinned, the meat of which he had consumed. He then went into his cave, took his bone implement which he fashioned from the same deer, danced himself into exhaustion, went into a trance for three days and received a vision from the gods of his tribe telling him where the herds would be this winter.

Recovering from his trance, he told the hunters where to find the herd and assured them that the gods would grant them a good hunt with no deaths. The hunters found the herd where it was supposed to be, killed a number of them with only a few injuries to the hunters, and returned triumphantly to the tribe which would have food for the winter.

Fast forward 10,000 years. A wannabe shaman puts on a deer hide, antlers, and bone implement that he has fashioned from things that someone else killed which he bought at a store for money. He goes to a gathering on a Saturday night, which is the only time he can get off from work. He puts on the costume, dances for an hour or two, gets drunk, has feelings of arousal and energy which make him feel good, then drives home to sleep it off in a soft, warm bed.

The next day, he buys meat wrapped in plastic at the supermarket. Monday morning, he goes back to the real world and goes back to his real job, the job which feeds, clothes and shelters him and those who depend upon him. He works at his job but looks forward to the next convenient time when he can perform the ritual again.

Maybe there are superficial similarities between the two. Certainly, the wannabe shaman might go to great lengths to do the research to ensure that his costume and his chant is as authentic as possible, but there is something that has vanished during the course of the millennia between these two antlered dancers: consequences.

Our modern would-be shaman could spend his Saturday night watching television. It wouldn't matter – to him or anyone else. No tribe would starve, no hunters would return empty-handed trying to find a herd, or having found the herd, would make no kill, and maybe lose a hunter to injury or death. Nothing was accomplished by his actions. His dancing and drumming were a game, mere entertainment. It possibly stirred up primal energies in his repressed, 21st century, techno-geek self, which felt good for a while until he had to return to his day job, but ultimately no one was served. Not even him.

Ultimately, the energy that he raised which caused all the good feelings becomes the end in itself rather than the means to an end. So, he returns time and time again to the gathering to go through the whole thing again, but like an opiate causing artificial euphoria, it isn't real. It is a sham. The real energy that our ancestors stirred up that was vital to their survival now has no purpose, no outlet other than his own personal gratification.

Once the energy is stirred up, it needs a purpose. 10,000 years ago, it had a very important purpose: the survival of the tribe. Now, all it does is entertain, and eventually feed an addiction for a level of excitement and intensity that our modern world has lost.

It hasn't been that long in the cosmic scheme of things since our world was turned from an agrarian one to an industrial one when we as a culture traded in our subsistence farming with its dependence on the vagaries of natural cycles for the more predictable income that a factory could provide.

In America, in particular, it has only been a hundred years or so since our muddy streets were paved with asphalt, our horses, and mules replaced by cars and trucks, our houses and office buildings turned into hermetically sealed fortresses against wind, rain, and insects, and our diseases cured by antibiotics and other modern medicines. Very few people, even Pagans, are able to endure life without these comforts even for the length of a weekend camp out.

Consequently, in the process of conquering nature and its attendant problems, most modern adherents of the Craft are drawn to the worship of the gods of nature with absolutely no idea of what kind of nature they are gods of. They know they have lost something, a vital and visceral part of themselves. However, they don't know what that part is or how to get back in touch with it. In The Craft Today, published in Pentagram Magazine in 1964, Robert Cochrane wrote:

> *"...the Craft has rapidly become an escape hatch for all those who wish to return to a more simple form of life and escape from the ever-increasing burden of contemporary society. In many cases the Craft has become a funkhole, in which those who have not been successful in solving various personal problems hide, while the storm of technology, H-bombs, and all the other goodies of civilization pass by harmlessly overhead. Modern Witchcraft could be described as an attempt by twentieth-century man to deny the responsibilities of the twentieth century."*

In a desperate and sincere attempt to regain our connection with nature, we have instead reconstructed a plastic diorama of nature, an illusion of being in nature without actually having to deal with the unpleasant natural things that propelled our grandfathers and great grandfathers into building our antiseptic industrial society in the first place. We want the beautiful, fun, and exciting bits of nature but none of the hard, unpleasant, and dangerous bits, and in the process, we have lost both.

Many years ago, we had a friend who lived on a farm in Wales. Every year, he would watch hordes of Londoners move to Wales, and he would try to predict how long they would last with none of the creature comforts of the city. Most of them didn't even last the winter. As soon as they felt the bitter cold in their bones with no furnace to turn on, felt the ache in their muscles after chopping wood and hauling it into the fireplace, felt the emptiness in their stomachs when the available food didn't fill it, they bailed and went back to civilized society.

After all, it wasn't as though there wasn't a civilized society for them to go back to. Unlike their ancestors, who had no choice but to make do with whatever circumstances they found themselves in, the would-be back-to-naturists had a choice to remain or leave, and they chose to leave.

There is nothing wrong with creature comforts. In fact, our ancestors worked very hard to devise ways to keep the more uncomfortable and dangerous aspects of nature at bay long enough to develop what we know as culture: art, music, literature, poetry and religious ritual. Once we are no longer in danger of being killed and eaten by predators or dying from hunger, disease or infection, or being incapacitated by natural disasters, we can turn our attention to other matters less concerned with bodily or tribal survival.

We can draw pictures on the walls of our caves. We can tell stories and sing songs of our ancestors and eventually write them down for future generations to read. We can track the motion of the stars and navigate our way across oceans. We can spend time and effort making jewelry, ornaments, and things of beauty. We can develop codes of law and government. We can sow seeds and reap them and turn them into bread. We can selectively breed herds of animals with increased capabilities for nourishment and labor. We can develop medicines that cure illness. We can build cities. We can invent machines that will do our labor for us, that will convey us from one end of the continent to the other, that will fly through the air, that will perform complex calculations almost instantly. We can go to the moon.

However, this freedom from nature's dangers has led to nature becoming romanticized. Over the last hundred years, an entire film genre has grown up dedicated to anthropomorphizing animals, particularly dangerous animals. This goes beyond the occasional heartwarming story of devoted domestic animals such as cats, dogs or horses doing heroic, lifesaving deeds.

Cartoons such as those produced by Disney gave animals, especially wild animals, human characteristics, and emotions, making them kind, sweet, innocent and fun-loving instead of fierce and bloodthirsty. They talk, sing, dance and get along with each other and share like well-behaved kindergarteners.

This admittedly is standard children's fare and has been for many centuries. However, in the past, children would balance out the tales of talking animals with interaction with actual animals. They would eventually discover that the horse that drew the milk cart, the cow in the field across the road, the mice that lived in the roof thatch and the cat that caught the mice, and even the wolf that lurked on the edge of the forest not only didn't talk or sing, but didn't like humans and actually harmed them if provoked.

They also didn't get along with each other very well. The cat that chased the mice didn't dance and sing with them. It eventually caught, killed and ate them often leaving blood and mouse parts all over the floor. As they grew up, such children learned the difference between the story and the real world.

However, many children in our modern era don't learn that lesson quite so well. They not only hear stories about friendly talking animals, they see the cartoons on television and in the movies, and there are few real animals in the everyday life of most modern children to counteract the cartoon message.

After a certain age, most children will know the difference between a cartoon and real life, at least on a conscious level. On an unconscious level, however, not so much. Increasingly for most people what constitutes the real life of animals is what they see in zoos and on television in carefully filmed and edited documentaries which portrayed wild animals just like they were in the cartoons as tame and friendly to humans – just like dogs or cats.

This was particularly true for the kinds of animals which used to be considered enemies of humanity. Once, they were creatures that inspired terror. If a large predator could jump out of the bushes at any time and snare us, we were concerned only with staying out of its clutches. It was only when we had learned to live in caves and tamed the awesome power of fire that we were able to ensure our own safety and draw pictures of them instead.

The less and less we were subject to their predation, the more pictures we could draw and the more stories we could tell about them. They became remote, distant. Their threat was minimized until finally, we saw them in person only behind bars or glass in a zoo or in an animal park, and we had the luxury of admiring them, of choosing to care for them or exterminate them as it suited us. We became the predator and they the prey, and they inspired terror no longer.

Take the lion: King of the Jungle and predator par excellence. Even today in parts of Africa, hunting and killing a lion which is ravaging a village and killing and eating the most vulnerable members of that village constituted a test of courage for the local warriors. At the risk of life and limb, a warrior will defeat the lion, kill it, then dress in its skin and claws as a kind of blood rite. Through the control and discipline of his own predatory nature, he has defeated the lion and is now entitled to command its power to aid him in his next battle.

Travel to a large urban area in Europe or America. A would-be warrior fashions a mask of a lion (inspired by images taken from photographs) and puts it on. In a ritual on a Saturday night in between work weeks, he summons the spirit of the lion and attempts to identify with it. Since he has never even seen a lion in the wild, much less killed one, all he can do is pretend to be a lion for a while.

The problem is that he has no idea how a lion really behaves. The closest he has come to this kind of feline predatory energy is to keep a house cat. The predatory energy of the lion is foreign to him and is something he has no legitimate use for. At best, nothing happens and he plays an entertaining and ego-gratifying game for a few hours or years. At worse, it unleashes a power within him that he has not learned to control and he causes others harm. This is particularly the case if the person wearing the animal mask is exercising some kind of authority over others, such as John describes. What does wearing an animal mask and the power it presumably carries confer upon the wearer that he can't achieve as a human?

In the case of the African warrior who has summoned and controlled his own predator instinct, assuming the power of the lion is advantageous since he belongs to a culture that dictates that he must hunt and kill to eat and provide for his tribe.

The process of hunting is dangerous. The hunter could, and often does, get injured and then turns into prey himself. The power of the lion carries a price. The hunter must acknowledge that his encounter with the lion could have just as likely resulted in his death rather than the lion's, and the next encounter might very well turn out that way. He and the lion are equals; today, the lion lost, and the hunter wears his hide. Tomorrow, it might be the other way around.

The 21st-century urban shaman has not earned the right to command the power of the animal. He has risked nothing, sacrificed nothing to obtain the power, so the power commands him. He might actually become a channel for predatory power, but since he has no prey animals to use the energy on, he turns on members of his own species who have something that he wants or that he considers a threat to him and herein lies the problem.

Perhaps there is nothing so iconic in the popular imagination regarding witches as their ability to turn themselves into animals and fly off and do a lot of things that they couldn't do in human form. Legends from all cultures abound in shamans taking on animal form and traveling abroad, usually at night. Sometimes the shaman would take the form of predators – wolves, foxes, hawks, eagles. Other times, they were everyday animals that would be able to come and go without anyone really noticing them – ravens, hares, cats or dogs.

It isn't difficult to see where this legendary ability comes from. It comes from the folk memories of shamans dressing up in often elaborate animal costumes. The dancing and drumming served to put the shaman into a trance, and the costume he wore served to add the hypnotic suggestion that he should act like the animal he was portraying. So, he does – to the point where he convinces not only himself but others as well.

∼

About Journey to the Castle

In the summer of 1982, two idealistic and naive California witches embarked on a quest to find the source of a tradition that had come down to them seven years earlier, fragmented and distorted from a teacher who had himself received it in like manner.

An opportunity presented itself to travel to England to explore the roots of the tradition and they found that the roots did indeed grow deep in the soil that contained within it some very tainted elements.

In Journey to the Castle, Ann Finnin recounts the story of this journey, with all of its good, bad and ugly elements, whitewashing nothing and no one, least of all herself. What the reader comes away with is a frank commentary on the nature of religious and

spiritual movements with all of their enlightenment and pitfalls and how human nature can distort even the loftiest of teachings into a means of control and exploitation. This book is one couple's journey into the underworld. The author sincerely hopes

that her and her husband's experiences will serve to provide a warning to some and a solace to others who have engaged on a similar journey with less than desirable results and finally what the future holds for those with the courage and the honesty to embark on such a journey.

"Journey to the Castle is an insider's story of one of the less-known branches of Traditional Witchcraft, the Clan of Tubal Cain. Ann Finnin traces its rituals and teachings back to the charismatic but tragic 1960s English Witch Robert Cochrane and to his contemporary, the influential magician William Gray. She peels away later accretions to give readers the original teachings and goals while describing her and her husband's adventures and misadventures on the path to restoring the Clan in America."

- Chas S. Clifton, editor, The Pomegranate: The International Journal of Pagan Studies

About the Author

Ann Finnin has been active in magical groups since her first initiation in 1974. For the past forty-five years she and her husband Dave have run the Roebuck coven and continued to write about and teach witchcraft and related magical topics to a plethora of students. She and Dave live north of Los Angeles in an old house with a well-used, attached temple.

Journey to the Castle

by Ann Finnin

www.ingramcontent.com/pod-product-compliance
Lightning Source LLC
LaVergne TN
LVHW081355060426
835510LV00013B/1830